HOW WOULD YOU SURVIVE?

THE INCIDENT, THE ARREST, AND JAIL

A.J. Crenshaw, III

Acuité Media

HOW WOULD YOU SURVIVE? The Incident, The Arrest, and Jail

Acuité Media

Published by Acuité Media
Bowie, Maryland
Printed in the United States of America
First Printing Edition, 2022
ISBN: 979-8-9864653-3-3

DISCLAIMER

While the valuable content of this book is meant to help individuals navigate and survive the worse experience of their lives, the plethora of possible scenarios and personalities that a person can encounter in jail makes it impossible to provide a foolproof strategy or guarantee that any person can avoid being victimized or traumatized. Even as revised editions of this book are released in the future, there is always the possibility that some critical topic or scenario will be either omitted or lack specific details or descriptions. These advisements and principles prescribed in this self-help guide should be absorbed and utilized at your discretion based on your personality and unique encounters when and if you find yourself detained in jail.

Contents

Preface: No One Expected It

O n my mother's family portrait display is the face of a
beautiful baby boy with fine hair and big, bright, and
curious eyes. Like most parents, my mother and father instantly
adored and loved the beautiful face of their first-born creation
and began to imagine the great life that they hoped to provide
and prepare me for. The words "He's so bright" and "He's very
creative" became popular descriptions that my proud parents
heard as they watched me excel through elementary school and
be featured as God in a children's production of James Weldon
Johnson's *God's Trombones*. By age 12 my leadership qualities
evolved at my first job. By age 16, I was the youngest manager,
overseeing staff twice my age. Graduating ranked #4 in my high
school class yielded multiple scholarship offers including
employment incentives in the fields of technology and
journalism. Praiseworthy, I achieved being the first male of my
generation to attend college at a university.

No one imagined it. No one expected it. This popular computer science major would soon be transferred to the campus that merely resembled a college but was actually a correctional institution. No one expected that the beautiful baby boy with the big, bright, and curious eyes, the articulate and artistic, honor roll student would be exposed to influences and behaviors that would disrupt every facet of his life for years to come. Alike most of us, I never expected that one day I would actually go to jail, nor ever bear the stigma of a person who had been arrested or incarcerated. There was uncertainty that I would survive in prison, and honestly, I remember nights when I closed my eyes, prayed, and hoped to wake up in heaven instead of jail.

Amid episodes of depression, anxiety, and a stress-induced ulcer, many thoughts and questions filled my mind. Often, I asked myself, "How many people from all social classes and opportunities underestimate the possibility of going to jail? How many people have gone to jail having broken no law at all? How many of these people have witnessed others in jail being maimed, molested, and even killed?" In jail, there are people from every demographic background co-mingled. Some resort to being predators while others are victimized as prey. In either case, none of these former citizens had planned for their fate. They had no idea how to prepare for it and had no idea how to adapt to it.

Introduction: Too Close to Home, Too Often

Several hundred thousand people are arrested across the United States every year because crimes are occurring all day, every day. Most of these people never anticipated the possibility of being arrested. None of them are truly prepared for what awaits them on the other side of the fence, barbed wires, and concrete walls. Even those who have watched countless episodes of jail and prison reality shows cannot relate to the trauma and grief of the individual who wakes up every day in a real-life nightmare. Researchers debate over the approximate number of individuals in the U.S. who have been arrested in general. Some say 1 in 5 persons, 1 in 3 persons, and some say approximately seventy-seven million of the current 329 million persons living in the United States have a criminal record. Because some law enforcement jurisdictions in the U.S. still do not report all their arrest data to the FBI to be included in the annual Uniform Crime Reporting (UCR) Program no one can be certain whether the actual number is 23%, 30%, or higher. Neither is the relevant point. The relevant point is that there are thousands of people arrested every day who never expected to ever be arrested and/or go to jail —some report that an arrest is made every 3 seconds.

Where you live may place you at either a higher probability or a lower probability of being arrested. Sorry to say, but the color of your skin or ethnicity can realistically instigate whether you are randomly suspected of a crime and/or arrested. Your socioeconomic class and education level can too often influence whether you go to jail and for how long. You can easily be arrested because of who you associate yourself with in any environment or setting, regardless of your background, because bad associations can increase your chances of being seduced into risky activities and labeled guilty by association.

The most foolish thing that any of us can do is to take for granted the possibility of being arrested and even sent to jail. As human beings, we have an innate tendency to take risks and gamble with opportunities and temptations. We condition ourselves to believe that the worse will always happen to someone else. We all know many good people that have had many bad—and let us be honest-- illegal habits for many years. Because they have never been discovered or faced any consequences, we give them a pass and accept it as 'their normal' and ignore that their behavior is illicit. Maybe, that person is you. Any of these opportunities, habits, or flirtations with temptations can create a life-changing consequence. Neither your persuasive words nor tears will prevent you from being restrained by tight handcuffs. That turning moment may come one day, in some shape or form, so proactively studying this book may very well save your life or the life of someone you care about.

Act Like You Know

While some people's blatant illicit lifestyle makes their fate predictable, when exposed, the covert habits of others catch us by surprise. For example, the odd kid on campus known as the weed connect, we all know that it is only a matter of time before they get caught. But things take a turn for the worse when we are shocked and saddened after hearing of the arrest of their customer, who was your neighbor's child, who played with your children, to whom you gave a graduation gift, and celebrated their scholarship receptions. They were like family. Now they are expelled, charged as an adult, caught in the middle of an investigation bigger than anyone expected, and strangely they are remanded with a bail set higher than anticipated, and the clock is ticking.

You knew that the TV and electronics 'hook-up' person would eventually get caught. They have sold televisions, tablets, laptops, earbuds, and all the good stuff for way too long to far too many people. They may have sold something to you or to friends and relatives that you introduced them to. Well, maybe not you, but someone else like you who never considered how the person responsible for accounting for all that missing inventory would be impacted. What can an unexpected incident look like? When you get a crushing phone call about the arrest of your relative for grand larceny. Oh, yes… that relative with that sweet corporate office job at-you guessed it-a major electronics distribution company; and guess whose manager they have been responsible for auditing the last 2 years? Yep, that cool, reliable electronics 'hook-up' person.

Some of you always sensed that there was something shady about that coach whose lifestyle did not seem to match his salary.

It was no surprise when hearing that the coach was placed under arrest. However, when phones rang off the hook alerting that one of your relatives was arrested in the investigation linked to the same coach, everyone was shocked.

Someone has worked hard for years, raising, supporting, providing, and sacrificing to give their children opportunities greater than they experienced for themselves. They acknowledged that they didn't live in the best community, and didn't have access to the best schools, but they prayed often that their sacrifices would pay off and their children would overcome, excel, and beat the odds. Since they can't be with their children all 24 hours of the day, they can only hope that their children will make good decisions. Yet, it is way too common that this scenario takes a hard turn, with a hard knock at the door, and a harsh authoritative voice on the other side with a search warrant in hand. There is an overwhelming flood of emotions at this moment, especially when it becomes clear that they are about to be held accountable for a loved one's actions after that harsh voice commands, "Please. Place your hands behind your back."

For years I have understood how essential the information in this book is for changing and even preserving the lives of people who may one day find themselves in a dark, embarrassing space called jail. I must admit that the need did not become urgent until I experienced having two family members both facing the possibility of being sentenced to serve jail time. What is portrayed on television and in movies has confirmed, for most people, that incarceration is a real penalty for committing crimes. The images are not pleasant, are not comfortable, and many of us find the illustrations appalling. The on-screen depictions are not exaggerating reality. Spending time in jail is traumatic to even the most level-minded individual. It can be described by some individuals as transitioning from a place of paradise to a place of torment. Entering jail is like entering a new dimension. You are certainly entering a new world with rules founded on restriction, power, control, and dehumanization. No one would wish this on a person that they cared for, much less themselves.

Several years ago, I sat in a restaurant on the opposite side of the table from one of my nephews. He listened intently to me as I watched him eat what would be the last satisfying meal before reporting to court for sentencing two days later. Maryland crab cakes and macaroni and cheese would leave a memorable flavor in his mouth, but it would be my words of wisdom that he would digest to help him preview the many challenges that he would face once he entered jail for the next few years.

I appreciated him calling and requesting to meet with me and expressing his admiration. So, I did not take his cry for help for granted. I felt as if I was his Obi-Wan Kenobi asked to unlock a level of insight that could help him endure his inevitable journey into the Sith Citadel. The toughest part of this conversation with my nephew was when I looked into his eyes and considered the possibility that this may be the last time that I ever see him again. I am by no means implying that I didn't intend to visit him, but rather accepting a hard truth. The hard truth is that once a person enters any jailhouse there are no guarantees. Too many individuals go into the jail system every year and lose their lives. Oftentimes it is by no fault of their own. On other occasions, they find themselves in situations that they could have avoided if they only had a bit more wisdom. The U.S. Department of Justice reported in their State and Federal Prisoner Mortality Statistics (2001-2018) that a combination of federal and state U.S. prisoner deaths reflected an increase of annual deaths from 3,170 in 2001 up to a pre-pandemic record high of 4,513 in 2018. These death tolls include the combination of suicides, homicides, drug-related deaths, and health-related deaths. The question is, "How could someone who is unfamiliar with such an environment, such an experience, apply the wisdom that it's only acquired through experience?" This wisdom of the jailhouse Jedi is stored in the minds and hearts of many correctional officers, prison staff, or inmates who have spent several years in what is officially a mental and physical war zone (prison). Many of them have been tried, tested, and proven to have not only successfully coped, but also to have strategically survived.

Once my nephew finished his meal, he began to express to me his biggest concerns about going to jail. Much of it was related to estimating how long he would be gone in addition to safety concerns and the possibility of getting into conflicts. I explained that the length of time that he would serve will truly depend on the stipulations of his sentencing. A crucial factor would be how well he is able to navigate through all the distraught personalities that he would encounter that could hinder his ability to receive an early release. He reminded me of his temperament and how he tends to get into conflicts. He claimed that his conflicts are always with people who, for no good reason, just don't like him. I explained to him, as I'm about to describe to you, some of the first tools needed in preparing your mind when and if things take such a turn south and you actually are taken to jail.

For some of us, it may seem like Lady Justice is peeking and not seeing our situation clearly and fairly. There are too many communities of underprivileged and undereducated children born into cultures gullible for criminal activity. They grow up as fuel to a hungry fire, fools in a game with a hidden manual, and primed for prison. Although this group of minorities (predominantly African Americans and Latinos) disproportionately assume the majority of prison beds, we have recently been reminded that the same handcuffs have been placed on the wrist of Ivy League school graduates, a presidential campaign chairperson, a presidential campaign foreign policy advisor, a former national security advisor, former CIA agents, celebrities, politicians, professional athletes, priests, pastors, police officers, deaf, blind and even mentally impaired persons. In either case, the most foolish thing that any of us can do is to take for granted the possibility of a loved one --or ourselves-- being arrested and even sent to jail.

> *Note: Throughout this text, jail and prison may be used synonymously. Although jail is commonly referred to as a pretrial facility where people are detained either after their arrest, until their court date, or for short term sentences, every inmate is subjected to all of the same hazards and risk in a jail as they would while serving a longer sentence in a prison.*

Your Harsh Reality

You have just taken the first step into a harsh reality. What you have in your hands is considered a reference book for many, a self-help book to most, a training manual, and even a survival kit for a multitude. You are welcome to enjoy what has become a treasure, especially for people who live in the United States which houses 25% of the world's prison population. Now, more than ever, most people carry a bit of anxiety about one day being arrested for no good reason. Others declare that they can imagine being arrested for a good reason such as for protesting or protecting someone or something that they are passionate about or love.

Fact: Individuals wrongfully convicted in the United States spend an average of 9 years in prison before being exonerated? In 2015, the Washington Post reported in an article *The staggering number of wrongful convictions in America* that "the vast majority of innocent defendants who are convicted of crimes are never identified and cleared." Neither the innocent nor the guilty would have predicted a future that included their being arrested or incarcerated.

Innocent and guilty people share everything in common once they have been arrested and incarcerated. You face the same treatment by guards, the same rules and regulations, the same dangers of being victimized, and the same desperate need to survive, cope, and hopefully make it out of jail in reasonably good condition. So, let these pages prepare, enlighten, and guide you through what may prove to be the most challenging time of your life.

Kimberly Long

Profile: Nurse and mother of 2 youth
Year of Arrest: 2005; appealed
conviction upheld in 2008
Offense: Murder of life partner found
on their couch with severe head injuries
Sentence: 15 years to Life in Prison
Conviction vacated by Supreme Court
after serving over 7 years in prison
due to fake evidence being used to
convict her.

Chapter 1: Take The Reality Test

If you cannot pass this initial test of this chapter, please stop reading and consider checking yourself in at the nearest psychiatric hospital. Treatment may only be possible through a counselor or a close encounter of the third kind. You may have to be abducted by the truth.

Here we begin the initial training designed to help in keeping people alive, change the pattern of some people's behavior for the better, soften the hearts of many, and confirm a seldomly acknowledged system of discrimination and exploitation. It should restore broken hearts and hope between some family members and may keep someone from committing suicide.

Before you can really appreciate this book, you must make note of a few things. So, let us set the ground rules.

✓ Do not lie to yourself.
✓ Do not fool yourself.
✓ Do not deceive yourself.

Who Are You?

At the end of each chapter in this book are case summaries of popular and not-so-popular people. But who are you? Do you have a reflection in the mirror? Are you a human being living on the marvelous planet earth? Do you have immunity i.e., a free pass to break laws without getting penalized?

Knowing who you are is essential for helping you to transparently face the realities of karma, chance, and coincidence. Sadly, some people become so high-minded and over-clothed in their success that they do not believe anything can happen to them. They are like aliens. They function in their own world, their own rules, and their own reality. When they encounter situations that force them to accept that they are just like everyone else, they oftentimes resort to acting as if they are stupefied with classic responses. "This can't be happening to me!" "This is some kind of a mistake!" "I don't understand!" "I didn't know!"

Who are you? Are you immune to the common cold or incapable of getting sick? You can smoke, smoke, and smoke carefree with confidence that smoking will negatively affect everyone else's body but yours. Maybe you notoriously and proudly jaywalk and dare any driver to act like they don't see you and run you over. Maybe you are the child or relative of someone affluent, popular, or influential and you've been conditioned to take nothing seriously except what you can financially benefit from. You believe that nothing can hurt you, that you have nine lives, that you are privileged, that you could "stand in the middle of Fifth Avenue and shoot somebody, and not lose any voters"- no pun intended.

Do you ever look in the mirror to do more than admire yourself? Have you ever just stared at your reflection and considered that your entire face could be altered in the sudden moment of a freak occurrence or accident? Have you ever imagined how you would look with facial burns, scars, a missing eye, or deformed lips?

Have you ever stared at the sky, the hills, the land, and buildings or trees around you and acknowledged that you are on this planet just for a time and most of these wonders will be here for generations to come minus yourself?

Are you one of those fictional, lucky charm characters who has never been in any kind of trouble, drama, conflicts, or experienced loss or misfortune? You have never told a lie; never kept or taken something that did not belong to you (stolen). Never kept a secret for someone who did something wrong, never failed to come to a complete stop at a stop sign, never cursed at someone, or never discretely passed gas in an occupied room and did your best to act oblivious? Now that I have your attention and you are considering which one of us is a little crazy, let's take a closer view.

Top 10 things you have in common with every other human being

1. You will die someday. (Sorry to start so strong, but it's true)
2. You bleed red blood.
3. You <u>can </u>get sick.
4. You are not invincible.
5. You have free will. (ability to choose to do right or wrong)
6. You take risks.
7. You <u>cannot</u> be <u>totally</u> trusted.
8. You will break rules, and laws, and/or will challenge some authority figure.
9. You can get arrested.
10. You can go to jail.

Many people carelessly ignore numbers 1-4 and are either in denial of 5-10 or have been habitually lying to themselves about them all. If you are one of these people brace yourself because the big hand of reality will soon slap good sense into you. One of our most common human tendencies is that we will spend moments each day (every day) fantasizing about something that is wrong legally or morally. Like slapping the hell out of your boss or teacher, or server—just keeping your attention. Why? Because we just can't help ourselves. We have a deficiency that no human can cure called *cantgitrite*. In your mind, you will want, desire, and covet something or someone that does not belong to you. You *will* think of hurting someone. If angry enough, you will imagine killing someone. Evil desires go through a process in our minds like becoming impregnated. The desire is conceived (like a child in a womb) and it will either miscarry i.e., be erased from our imagination before it is fully developed; or it will fester and bring forth the birth of a tsunami that will devastate someone's life.

Confession

Now that your mind is open, let's open that heart. We do not need a real doctor, priest, or minister at this moment. What you are about to expose will be kept in the strictest of confidence. These bright pages will symbolize the doctor, priest, or minister. The dark letters will symbolize your dark truths. A doctor takes you into his care and performs tests in hopes of relieving your illness. A priest/minister takes you into his confessional or sanctuary, listens, meditates, and prays over both you and your situation. All this is to relieve your heart and mind of your burdens. Both reach for the truth to provide a solution. Can you handle the truth?

The truth is that many people saw the title of this book and immediately felt like it either did not apply to them, it was of no interest or use to them, or they felt that the idea of being arrested or going to jail is beneath them. Yet, they could be driving home from church, from a family gathering, from work, from shopping, from picking up the kids, heading home from a party, or driving home after a couple of drinks, and the moment that a police car pulls behind them with lights flashing, they become uncomfortable. Isn't the unknown uncomfortable, the unpredictable, and the fact that in those next few moments they have to be humble and submit to an authority that just interrupted their day? In such moments most people today wonder if they should pull out their phones and start recording. They begin anticipating what may potentially be about to happen or what the officer thinks that they have done. This could be a quick, easily resolved situation or if they honestly know that they are at some fault, this encounter can wreck their day or worse. Now that we agree that no one is exempt from, in the least, being accosted by the police, let's move on.

Look back over your life, your yesterday, or even your today. Think of three things that you have done wrong that, if you had been caught, you could have been arrested for. Put down this book for a moment and just think......

Now, although I asked you to think of three things, it only takes one of these instances, one arrest, one conviction to change your life forever. Three convictions in some states could get you sentenced to life in prison. If you are thinking, "but mine wasn't that serious." Wrong answer. If it were illegal or immoral, it was serious, otherwise, you would not have considered it to be wrong in the first place. When you reach a point in your life when you become so comfortable doing wrong just because you don't think that the offense is that serious, you are planting seeds into your own mind that will encourage you to take greater risks in due time. In time the world will hear your pitiful cry, "this can't be happening to me," "this is a mistake," "I don't understand," "It wasn't me," "I made a mistake," and "I didn't know!"

If you cannot think of one thing that you have done that would have warranted your arrest, pinch yourself, slap yourself, splash a cup of ice-cold water in your face, or whatever it takes to keep me from doing it to you. You had better be so young that you barely understand the words that you are reading. Otherwise, if you are twelve years old or older, we are going to try this again.

Look back over your life, your yesterday, or even your today. Think of one (1) thing that you have done or considered doing wrong that, had you been caught, you could have been arrested for. Yes, this time I added 'or considered doing wrong' because under the right pressure, stress, anxiety, fear, or anger you can temporarily lose your mind, and what you 'considered doing' will take shape right before your very eyes, by your own hands. For those of us who do not understand the law or still do not believe the diagnosis - that we are all infected with *cantgitrite* - allow me to dig deeper into your conscience.

Let's refer to this next chapter---Four (4) examples of "Why you may get arrested for dummies"

Saurabh Chawla

Profile: eBay merchant
Year of Arrest: 2022
Offense: Conspiracy; interstate transportation of stolen goods, and tax evasion. Over a 5 year period bought stolen packages from FedEx and stolen iPods from school employees and resold them on eBay and Amazon.
Sentence: 5 years and 6 months in prison.

Felicity Huffman

Achievements: Primetime Emmy Award Winner: Outstanding Lead Actress in a Comedy Series *Desperate Housewives*
Year of Arrest: 2019
Offense: Conspiracy to commit mail fraud and honest services mail fraud for paying an admission consultant $15,000 to have a proctor correct her daughter's SAT answers.
Sentence: 14 days in jail; $30,000 fine, supervised release; 250 hrs community service.

Chapter 2: Why You May Get Arrested For Dummies

We can truly draft another whole book describing why everyone and anyone has the potential to get arrested. For now, for those who still think the possibility is farfetched, we will just write an excerpt of how dumb it is to believe that you could never be arrested.

Example 1: We Are Emotional Beings

It is believed that we have at least 27 categories of emotions. We are the ultimate emotional beings. Regardless of how social you are, whether you are outgoing and enjoy interacting with people, or you are very reserved and only socialize when you must, you still have feelings. In every setting, in some way, you must interact with another person with who you are not in control of. That other individual also has feelings. Whenever feelings are activated, there is the potential for conflict.

For example, we shop or beg for all our necessities including our food and clothing. We pay for amenities, a service, or a product with money that we earn from our jobs. Let someone 'mess with' or 'mess up' our money that we need on time. "What. I'm not getting paid?" "Excuse me. This is not all of my money!" Do you see how you feel right now just imagining one of these scenarios? Some of us would lose our religion when confronting someone about our money. Even the most reserved and diplomatic, intellectual could reach a breaking point when you are confronting a situation so sensitive and significant as your money. In this scenario, you are at the mercy of how the other person responds to you. The more uncooperative, indignant, or carefree they are about timely addressing your need to receive what is rightfully yours (your money), the more vulnerable you are to responding in a manner that may require the police to intervene. Once the police get involved, what happens next totally depends on how the officer(s) feel about the situation and how they feel about the attitudes of the people involved.

We must emphasize that everyone--I do mean every last breathing person--has a breaking point, a last button, a last nerve, a point of no return, that point where our anger management malfunctions. It is the point we pray that no one pushes us to. The point that will unleash the Beast. That beast that lays dormant in each of us awakens after a situation spikes our blood pressure and adrenaline overwhelms our nervous system so much that in the aftermath, we convince ourselves that we blacked out. We can be driven so completely out of character that we can find ourselves standing before a judge who believes that we are and will always be the beast; and, the best possible exorcism is to spend some time with the jail chaplain.

In the earlier paragraph opening, I intentionally noted that some of us beg for our necessities because panhandling for a living is real among individuals that are homeless--or who pretend to be homeless. In either case, panhandlers have feelings too. Those who are genuinely destitute often have suffered traumatic circumstances that now force them to stand in traffic and beg for help from strangers which can also be traumatizing. Imagine a homeless person, on a sweltering day, hungry, and dealing with some minor mental health issue. This homeless person has subjected themselves to approaching people in their cars and not knowing what type of emotional state the drivers and passengers are in. Consider how quickly a brief interaction between both emotional beings can escalate into foolishness if either of them responds negatively. At every red light, the panhandler has been approaching the full spectrum of car types (from old 'just get me home cars' to luxury cars) for hours, in the hot sun, and has only received a total of 8 dollars and a bottle of Pepsi. Then some insensitive driver says, "No. Get a job like everybody else!" The homeless person instantly has a flashback of getting fired from their $65,000 a year job, which caused them to deplete their savings, max out their credit cards, their home foreclosed, their spouse leaves, and there was no true family to lean on but the people they later met in the shelter. The charge "No. Get a job like everybody else!" triggers a flood of emotions. This flood of emotions evolves into a verbal confrontation between the homeless person and the occupants of the car who threatens to slap them or run them over. That escalates to police intervention.

It can quickly go downhill from here for all parties involved. This is not just a scenario. This is real-life stuff that happens every day across our country.

Every day we find ourselves at the mercy of another person's emotional state either at home, at work, at church, shopping, driving, or walking down the street. Remember the rude cashier or server? The one that couldn't count money; the one who tried to talk to you like you were stupid instead of giving you good customer service; the cashier or receptionist who lied saying, "I'm sorry. There is nothing that I can do. You can call corporate... Well, I am the manager..." Finish these statements with your own experiences and you can relate to how easily we can be baited or tempted into overreacting to a situation and finding ourselves trying to negotiate with the police. This brings us to example two.

Example 2: The Police Are Unpredictable Humans

Understand that all police officers are also human beings, flawed, and just as emotional as we civilians are. Even though police have been trained to not allow their emotions to obscure their ability to be fair and objective, they had personal lives before they started their careers in law enforcement and they still do. Their pre-law enforcement lives were full of experiences and influences that have shaped their personality and shaped their worldview. None of this gets deleted by the police academy. The police uniform, and the symbol of power and authority that it breathes, will enhance either the good or bad attributes of the person who wears it. An individual who is empathetic, sympathetic, and fair-minded may strive to use their role as an officer to have a positive impact on their community. An individual who has not been raised in a culturally diverse community or who has not been even educated in culturally diverse institutions will not immaculately become multiculturally sensitive once they put on a police uniform. An individual who grew up with an inferiority complex, who was always trying to fit in and be accepted, was always gullible and easy to influence, will not put on a police uniform and immediately begin to think interdependently and feel included. They will adopt the mentality and practices of the group of officers who they believe will fill their void of feeling inadequate.

The police uniform does not erase personal frustrations, trauma, grief, heartache, financial stress, family conflicts, or any other life issues that we all share. Police officers, in their humanity, consciously or unconsciously experience displacement and projection. Displacement is a classic defense mechanism. It is the act of taking negative actions against someone other than the real person that you have an issue with. For example, it is when an officer gets angry at their teenage kid for getting suspended from school and instead of sternly disciplining their child the patrolling officer stops their car and harasses the first group of youth that they see walking down the street. It is the officer who is reprimanded by their superior and because they fear the consequences of being insubordinate, they begin randomly pulling over drivers without cause and to blow off steam. You or your child may be one of those youth that is targeted. You may be one of those antagonized drivers. Taking someone to jail may be the only coping mechanism that some officers have developed.

Projection is attaching to others those feelings that you have not dealt with about yourself. An officer who habitually lies to everyone in their personal life may always act as if everyone else is lying to them. A police officer's belief that you are lying, leads to a belief that you have something to hide, which leads to suspicion, which implies probable cause in their minds, which could escalate to you being arrested for no good reason.

There is no doubt that every single day, someone is arrested for no other reason than they just happened to run into the wrong police officer who was having a bad day. That officer's only coping mechanism was to displace his frustrations upon you.

Example 3: Criminality Is A Culture For Many

Over 37 million people in the United States are considered poor based on a 2021 census report. Poverty-stricken Americans populate segments of cities and counties throughout the nation. Having the worst schools is normal for many of them. Having substandard living conditions is common for many of them. Having to share clothes among family members is not unusual. Being in and out of unemployment is oftentimes frequent. Having little to no healthy food throughout the month and never experiencing the world beyond their neighborhood is normal for many of them. Their most important priority is merely surviving. Their daily chore is maintaining or gaining possession of the bare necessities to survive with far less income or economic resources than more fortunate Americans.

Our poverty-stricken neighbors live in our nation that aggressively commercializes images that seduce lower-class labeled citizens into desiring materials too expensive for them to comfortably acquire. As a result, they are conditioned to be materialistic; so, they struggle to acquire products that will momentarily provide them with gratification, pleasure, and relief from despair. Some will prioritize buying expensive shoes, clothing, and hairstyles while their refrigerator sits nearly empty in a house or apartment that they don't own. It is sad to see a person wearing a nearly $200 pair of sneakers and not even have a real bed to sleep on. Many of these communities that have the lowest incomes and economic resources pitifully have the easiest and greatest access to expensive drugs and alcohol. Some resort to self-medicating themselves with substances to cope with their daily struggle. To steal, to rob, to sell drugs, to act out while under the influence of substances, to distrust, to be easily incited, to dislike school, to strive to possess what television, movies, and music shape their minds to desire, is the culture of criminality that too many beautiful children are involuntarily born into. Too many children are groomed to indulge in criminal activities as a means of not just their survival but to help meet the needs of individuals in their household.

Unfortunately, the culture of criminality is further bolstered by our mentally delicate youth who fill beds in the nation's 1,566 juvenile correctional facilities. The likelihood of an arrested youth being confined in a detention center has remained approximately 1 in every 3 for the last 15 years, despite juvenile justice reforms and consistent declines in youth confinement rates. Yes, this sounds contradictory, so let's clarify. Based on the latest data (2019), although a much smaller number of youth offenders are being confined in juvenile correctional facilities, any youth who face a judge today are just as likely to be confined as those that faced a judge in 2005. Unfortunately, there is still far more youth being confined for minor offenses than for serious offenses, especially youth who are Black or Native American.

Showcased on mantles, bookshelves, walls, photo albums, and social media posts are millions of adorable images of infants and toddlers that proud parents display and share so that others will also relish the joy of their creation. Few parents, if any, foresee the image of their children, 14 plus years later, displayed among a database of naive juvenile offenders.

One of the most mortifying feelings for a parent is certainly produced at the moment that they receive notification that their child has been arrested. Even for those parents who privately admit that their child isn't an angel--a bit headstrong, hardheaded, having mastered the art of knowing everything but haven't lived long enough to know much of anything—they may instantly worry and stress over the thought of their child being mishandled or manhandled in jail.

No matter how much we attempt to teach our children right from wrong and attempt to drive foolishness out of their hearts before they leave our house, they may be at a higher risk of being the dummy to get arrested than we are. It has been scientifically proven and agreed upon by the U.S. Supreme Court that adolescents take more risks and are far less likely to exercise good and rational judgment than an adult would according to the "developing brain theory." Because juveniles are considered cognitively less responsible for committing the same crimes that adults do, not only can they no longer be condemned to life sentences, but sentencing guidelines are universally beginning to yield to more age-appropriate treatment options for juvenile offenders. I must emphasize, 'beginning to yield' because there remain mixed feelings among judicial, political, legislative, and community leaders over how to hold youth accountable when their offenses are considered egregious. Meanwhile, youth justice advocates reiterate that the youth don't have the capacity to fully understand the repercussions of their actions. Our 16- to 17-year-old youth are at risk of facing the harshest sentences because research has noted that the conduct and decision-making of youth in this age range, the maturity gap years, is highly influenced by social acceptance, and thrill-seeking, and places them at the highest risk of reoffending.

Without getting too technical let's summarize the science for our cynical readers. According to research from the National Institute of Mental Health, around the age of 12, adolescent brain cells begin to rewire themselves starting from the back of the brain and working their way to the front of the brain. The back of the brain, where memory and emotions are processed, matures faster while the front of the brain, where decision-making and impulses are regulated slowly develops until approximately age 25. The best analogy that I have read is by a psychologist, David Walsh, who describes a youth's brain as like a fully functional car accelerating with no brakes. A teenager who biologically has less good sense and is more easily influenced to commit offenses is like a smoldering fire. This is not to imply that our children are completely incapable of making sound decisions, assessing risk, and controlling their impulses because many of our youth truly display a higher level of maturity than others. However, research notes that in comparison to adults, our teens' decision-making is compromised when their less mature frontal lobe (front region of the brain) experiences highly emotional or intense peer pressure situations. What does adding fuel to that fire look like?

Adding fuel to the fire looks like impairing the development of the front of an adolescent's brain with drugs and alcohol. Then add another douse of fuel made up of negative influences and adverse experiences. These experiences manifest within and outside of an adolescent's household including uncensored music, video games, and social media, unhealthy relationships, residing in disadvantaged neighborhoods, or growing up in a privileged environment that inadvertently instills entitlement and little accountability.

Too many of our underprivileged and underserved youth may never be equipped to overcome the environments and influences that condition them to lack ambition. Some youth are haunted by generations of underachievement that have been used to develop and normalize the culture of criminality which fuels a pipeline to prison. Going to jail is, as a result, a rite of passage for many youth and young adults. Some people utilize jail as a therapeutic time-out or escape from the daily complications that accompany poverty. It is a dismal opportunity to be temporarily reunited with friends and relatives that are already on their jail hiatus. They precondition their minds to find no shame in declaring "When I go to jail..." acknowledging that the possibility of actually being arrested and taken to jail is not so farfetched.

Example 4: Guilty Until Proven That Somebody Messed Up

An article in the July 2022 edition of the *Pittsburg Post-Gazette* titled, "The travesty of innocence" highlighted that "criminologists and other experts estimate that from 2% to 5% of the nation's nearly 2 million prisoners are innocent." If we do the math, this estimation cryptically reveals an appalling truth that between 40,000 and 100,000 innocent citizens are incarcerated right now in the United States. This is an absurd spread of potentially 60,000 people. Whether it be an actual total of 40,000 or any number up to 100,000, it tragically represents a combination of thousands of mothers, daughters, fathers, sons, neighbors, best friends, etc. who woke up one morning with no idea or expectation that they would be unjustly branded as guilty and confined in prison until, **if** and when, someone realizes that a mistake was made.

Worse than being incarcerated, only because someone made the mistake of arresting you in the first place and ultimately convicting you, is when an officer falsely arrests you on purpose. Allow me to repeat my earlier proclamation that our country has many, many good cops that perform their job honorably. The only struggle that most of them have is facing their reluctance or fear of challenging and exposing their corrupt co-workers.

Every year some judge has to face the frustration of dismissing a handful of cases associated with a police officer and/or prosecutor's misconduct. This misconduct could look like an officer who is proven to regularly participate in crimes, an officer who has allowed their substance abuse to influence their decision-making on the job, to an officer or prosecutor who enjoys falsely arresting and convicting people to meet quotas. In 2020, the National Registry of Exonerations conducted a study of 2,400 cases of exonerated defendants that included incidents of groups of officers planting drugs or guns on defendants, concealing evidence that would prove a defendant's innocence, witness tampering, misconduct in interrogation, fabricating evidence and lying (perjury) during trials. These practices are not just exaggerated fiction from episodes of your favorite crime drama. Your favorite crime dramas are so good because they mimic real-life travesties of justice. It's good t.v. entertainment until you or someone that you care about becomes the real-life victim of (as the study described) a law enforcement culture that rewards reckless behavior, maintains ineffective leadership, and fails to petition for sufficient resources to conduct high-quality prosecutions and investigations.

By no fault of your own, you can be randomly subjected to accusations, arrest, and even worse, a wrongful conviction. You can be staring red-eyed at a cold jail cell wall trying to figure out how you will survive this unjust experience that has turned your world upside down. The National Registry of Exonerations reported in June of 2021 that they had accounted for over 25,000 years of freedom lost to 2,795 wrongfully convicted persons in America who spent an average of approximately 9 years in prison before being exonerated. A key observation to note is that these numbers do not include the many more cases that have yet to be discovered and reported.

Bobby Bostic

Profile: Began smoking and drinking at age 10; PCP use at age 13; arrested at age 16

Year of Arrest: 1995

Offense: Robbery, attempted robbery, armed criminal action, assault, and kidnapping

Sentence: 241 Years in prison and eligible for parole at age 112. Missouri laws passed in 2021 required parole hearings after 15 years of incarceration for individuals that committed crimes as juveniles "and serving 'de facto' life sentences for nonhomicide crimes." Bostic was paroled in December 2021 and scheduled for release on November 9, 2022.

Chapter 3: Stop Thinking That They Can't Come For You?

Bad boy, bad girl, watcha gonna do... watcha gonna do when they come for you? Run, resist, cry, play stupid, or genuinely look clueless as to why you are being jacked up. The most popular reason that so many people go to jail is that very few people who break the law expect to get caught. Some have gotten away with petty and even major crimes so often that they have convinced themselves that they can keep getting away with it. Some believe that they are skilled or gifted in committing specific crimes without remorse. Many of us are experts at keeping illicit secrets. These skeletons are still hidden and if they remain locked in our closet, unexposed, we are each at risk of repeating the actions, and at risk of hearing those haunting words, "You have the right to remain silent...!" -- that is, if you are fortunate. In some instances, you could be hearing those words while under duress. Most of us have seen some of the nicest people go crazy when they were approached by police officers, and they wound up getting slammed around and arms nearly broken during some officer's attempts to subdue and handcuff them. Sadly, some have not walked away from the encounter breathing.

"I can't believe this!" or some variation of that statement tends to roll off the lips of people who honestly thought that they would outsmart law enforcement indefinitely. Case in point, the FBI Uniform Crime Report reflects that every year since 2010 approximately 1.5 million people in the U.S. have been arrested for drug/illegal narcotics charges. Virtually none of those drug arrestees have gone to school to study criminology or forensics. They do not have the resources, knowledge, or time to effectively monitor the daily operations of the investigators to strategically avoid being caught. Law enforcement agents have made a career of studying people with the use of government-supplied resources and technology that enables them to spend all day and night "getting paid" to catch people who foolishly dare to think that they cannot or will not ever get caught.

I reiterate that *everyone* has on some occasion gambled with their wellbeing, their reputation, their livelihood, and even their very lives by indulging in some illicit activity. Activities range from lying to an authority, driving under the influence of alcohol, stealing time from their employer, to being in possession of some controlled dangerous substance, some bootlegged product, illegal information, or worse. Why? It is because we are bold, curious, and mischievous. We are considered the most reckless species on the earth, with this delirious, naïve belief that everyone gets caught, but us.

Martha Stewart, Bernie Madoff, and Felicity Huffman took risks of distinct types and likely none of them expected to get caught; and they certainly didn't expect to wound up in prison.

What we often fail to acknowledge is that every celebrity and every wealthy person are merely regular people like you and me who have excelled in their professions. Indeed, they are equally as capable of breaking the law and getting caught. They too are curiously reading this book, relating to its content, and agreeing that any person can ignore their good conscience or lose their better judgment when placed in challenging and tempting situations.

In the heat of a moment of rage or fear, after fury, and premeditation, and after an incoherent spell of intoxication, you realize that you have crossed the line and committed a reprehensible crime that you cannot erase. You cannot travel back into time and undo that action that will be an indelible stain in your history and may very well have recurring consequences that haunt you throughout your future. It is classic to hear of the criminal activities of others and declare, "Whaaaat!" and "They were crazy," or "Why would they do something like that?" Our emotions are frequently challenged and tested. We experience abuse, shock, trauma, and become overwhelmed with anxiety. The breaking point or the moment when we cannot handle another ounce of mess varies and changes in every person. No one can honestly say what they would or will not do under the duress and/or influence of heartache, rage, tension, or when under the influence of reaction-altering substances. If we allow ourselves to continue being transparent, we can admit that many of us have had moments where we imagined doing some very strange, destructive, spiteful, cowardly, and outright stupid things. Some of us can honestly relate to situations that triggered others who have committed reprehensible crimes. We recall when we were two seconds and one scream away from losing our minds in similar situations as well. Some people are at the edge, right now, and only require the right situation, the wrong words, "just one more time" and --BIP, BOP, BAM—life as we knew it is changed forever.

Apprehension: Watcha Gonna Do?

You have just been approached by the police. Either aggressively or casually, they have introduced themselves and interrupted your day and interrupted your life. Whether you are guilty of something or genuinely innocent, your emotions are suddenly incited with worry, agitation, or both. In a matter of moments, your authority over your own life has been hijacked by the police. How you respond in these early seconds will determine how good, bad, or worse you will be treated. A wrong move could lead to injury or even death. A wrong word could lead to being antagonized, violated, harassed, or injured.

You have seen it on television shows like "Cops" or the new age cable variations like Man Hunter, Highway Patrol, and Jacked. You have even seen it in movies and on the news and either you never thought that you would face this kind of crisis, or you prayed to never face it again. Even if you acknowledge that you may be a member of the National Crime Society with an accumulation of frequent flyer miles to and from jail, you are wishing that this moment wasn't really happening. What will you do? How will you respond? Typically, you're going to do one of the following:

A. Dig into your archive of lies and hope to find one or more lies that will allow you to slither out of this situation.

B. Start crying and pleading that you've done no wrong and that the police have made a big mistake. (This is like the lie in A with added drama.)

C. Run! This will make you look guilty, will irritate the police, and likely guarantee that you will be injured if caught. After you are caught, you will probably resort to A or B, or you will just keep resisting arrest and get beat up. (...There is a small chance that you'll get away and live to risk your freedom another day.)

D. Quickly decide who you are going to pass the blame on.

E. Play dumb. This is a variation of A (above). This may buy you some time if you are good; otherwise, police will see right through it and will become agitated by your attempt to insult their intelligence.

F. Become belligerent. You will curse, fuss, and try to intimidate the police into leaving you alone. In most towns and cities this will almost guarantee that you will be going straight to jail regardless of whether you are innocent or guilty. The bigger concern is whether you will be going to jail with or without scrapes and bruises.

G. Plead for Mercy. You are hoping that you have encountered the nicest police officers in town. You are hoping that they will be so convinced by your pitiful pleas of "I'll never do it again. I promise" and they will actually let you go. This is not impossible, but it rarely works.

H. Bribe or seduce the police. What are the chances that the police are corrupt, dirty, or even perverted? If this were some Netflix drama, you would be okay; but this is the reality where most of us are not rich enough or sexy enough to entice a good police officer into compromising their badge—but it is possible.

I. Say very little. You are guilty as sin, and you know that the less that you say the better your situation may be for now. Once you are arrested and, in a cell, you will spend hours imagining what would have happened if you had exercised options A thru H.

J. Contrarily, if you are cocky or arrogant you will surrender in the confidence that you will mock the police by being quickly released after they have processed you.

K. If you are innocent, you may go away quietly (very unlikely) and hope that the scales of justice are well-calibrated.

Some suggested that I should have included the option of peeing your pants but that normally does not happen before or during an arrest--if you're not drunk. Certainly, you will have plenty of opportunities to blow out your bladder later at your bail hearing, sentencing, or jail initiation.

Off You Go

Options A thru H did not work in your favor. You are being transported to the nearest processing and booking station. In the rear of the transport vehicle, you are experiencing what is called phantasmagoria – images and scenes of your life, people that you love, replays of your arrest, and previews of jail are all rapidly shifting across the screen of your mind. Many become religious in this moment of panic, but your cries for God go unanswered. You may be crying inside and maybe on the outside. You are having a tantrum and still cannot believe what is happening. Your entire life and all your responsibilities are rolling away like movie credits across your pupils. Your heavy heartbeat and perspiration confirm that this is not a dream. You wish that this were a mere moment in a nightmare. As you squeeze your eyes tightly, you are praying that you'll open them to find yourself awake at home. Sorry--- the police transport vehicle is bouncing over bumps, your handcuffs are uncomfortably tight, and you ARE going to jail!

In the next few hours, the lives of your friends and relatives will be disrupted by the news of your arrest and your relationships with them will be put to the test. Some people will be shocked and worried while others may not be so surprised. You may or may not get released. You may not receive a reasonable bail. You may be detained. You might get the privilege of making a phone call in a reasonable amount of time. Get ready to receive a variety of responses from friends and family including promises to help, frustrated excuses of why they can't help, or total abandonment (they hang up after they hear "This is a call from _____ at ... detention center).

You are now aboard the emotional rollercoaster that can truly make you sick to your stomach. A serving of worry, two shots of anger, a twist of fear, and a spray of shame on the rocks. Virgin or not, you are about to become the star of your own reality show. No one really cares about who you are or where you are from at this stage. The police have a job to do. They must process you and even ask you many questions like they ask every other assumed guilty person--until proven innocent.

Lights, Camera, Fingerprint

Showtime! You are the star, so if it seems like everyone is looking at you, they are. Not only are they looking at you, but they are judging you, taunting you, and trying to figure out what you did wrong. Some of your co-stars, the other individuals that are also under arrest, are giving you the look-over to determine whether you have a familiar face or not. Why? Well, because people in jail tend to experience a moment of temporary comfort when they realize that they are being booked with familiar faces. Everyone needs allies in jail. It is like the opening credits to a movie. When we see the names of familiar actors, we become more encouraged and anticipate good entertainment. The problem is that you do not know if your documentary will be classified as an adventure, drama, or horror story-- a comedy is out of the question. Some of the familiar faces that you and your peers seek may include the faces of adversaries. It is of extreme importance that you recognize them as soon as possible.

Hopefully, you noticed that in my list of movie categories, I excluded a romance or love story. It is important to be aware of the people around you consistently. Even during the initial jail processing stage, there may already be someone sizing you up or staring at you fantasizing. Keep reading and we will address that subject later because just as you think things couldn't get any worse, you may become the object of someone's desire. This is truly not sarcasm.

In this scene, you are like dirt. You either feel like dirt or you are being treated like dirt. Even if the processing officers are being cordial towards you, you truly are not important to them. Every day they perform the same routine of arresting and processing everyday people and adding them to a database of law offenders. It is not their responsibility to determine whether you are guilty or innocent; so, in the meantime, you will receive the same treatment as your co-stars.

You are hereby inducted into the Hall of Shame, and you will be providing your fingerprints and your photo regardless of how bad you look. Your face will be documented and unforgotten for many years to come. There is no time to fix your hair, makeup, or wipe dirt or blood from your face. You do not have to smile, but you will take the picture. Some authorities prefer that you don't smile. They may prefer that you look as evil as possible and that your mugshot appears intimidating. This way, if officers ever come to arrest you in the future and use this mugshot as a reference, you will look like a serious threat. They will take pride in feeling like they are going to take down a 'bad guy.'

How soon you complete the processing procedure varies greatly. It usually depends on staff availability, the time of day, and the number of other individuals also waiting to be processed. Consider yourself entering a new dimension. From this moment forward until this crisis is over – however long it takes for you to see the streets again—you are in a new dimension of time. Here, the minute's hand on the clock seems to have a 30-minute delay. When 60 minutes have passed, the clock seems to have only moved 30 minutes forward.

Some believe that the entire tedious process (from the moment that you are taken into custody, to booking, to seeing the bail commissioner or judge) is designed to compel you to deeply think about, and consider your actions, and the weight of the consequences. Your life may feel like a slide-show presentation, played in slow motion and the presenter is reading word for word fifty slides full of paragraphs about your arrest. It is supposed to be an inconvenience and an uncomfortable, bitter taste of torment. Now that you have been processed and feel less of a person than you did when you were brought in, get ready for a ride with major mental turbulence.

Your life as you once knew it has been transported into an alternate dimension. You are locked inside of a time capsule without a helmet, no cushiony seats, and no control panel. Your level of safety is questionable; this will be an uncomfortable experience especially since you have absolutely no control over your environment. The only thing that your frustrated eyes can focus on is the naked interior of a cell, or you may be in an overcrowded bullpen (a large holding cell that uncomfortably holds multiple people). It is either too cold or too hot. If you are fortunate enough to be in a small, rural town, you may be in your own private, cold cell alone. Too often you end up sharing space in a holding cell whose capacity is far less than the number of bodies in it. Always, someone doesn't smell very good. It may even be your own body odor that is contributing to the rancid formula of urine, feet, breath, mildew, farts, alcohol, fear, and frustration. You and the other pirates must await your fate here in the hull of the ship wherever space allows. You may be on a bunk, a slab of concrete, on the soiled floor, or laying alongside the toilet. Your back and bones ache, your arms and legs keep falling asleep, and you are struggling to not burst out a humiliating scream. As badly as you wish that this weren't happening, every scene of this nightmare is happening!

Likely, you have been stripped of your watch and a wall clock is intentionally out of your sight. Without a measurement of time, this experience stays in slow motion. Being in slow motion should help you focus on the details of everything around you. You feel like you are in captivity, and you pray that time would fast forward to the point that the door opens to release you. Right now, you would love to hear an echo of an officer calling your name to step out of the cell for anything—anything to get out of the cell just for a little while. The only thing that can begin lowering your stress levels is a feeling that positive progress is being made. The frustration is depressing, and you find yourself constantly thinking about how bad your arrest will be viewed in the eyes of not just your family and peers, but also in the eyes of the prosecutor, judge, and/or a potential jury. Your image, self-worth, and self-esteem are influenced by how your peers and closest relationships view your situation. Who will forsake you now? Who will support you despite the implications of your arrest?

If you are already on some form of probation or parole, you may as well start creating your "who will forsake me" list and pencil in the names of any judges or agents associated with your past cases. It is not personal. If you're not fortunate enough to be exonerated of these new charges, it is their job to be the wolves that you have been thrown to. Saving you may no longer be an option that takes precedence over saving the public from your alleged recklessness.

You are one phone call away from seeing which friends or relatives will be added to your "they'll forsake me, they'll forsake me not" list. Some of their genuine feelings about your situation will be hard to interpret once you initially tell your side of the story, especially if you are guilty. Guilty people oftentimes lie to family members, friends, and their attorneys, at least initially, to ensure as much support as possible. If you haven't needed anyone at all lately, that streak ends now. If you are allowed bail, someone's money or property must be sacrificed--yours or theirs. Whichever, you must rely on someone to convey what is required to a bondsman. Only you know what you need to do and say to motivate your potential supporters to help you. You can tell them the truth about your situation, or you can lie.

How Much Is Your Trouble Worth?

Bail is cash, a bond, or property that an arrested person gives to a court to ensure that if he or she is released they will appear in court when ordered to do so. Something that the bail review judge considers when determining if you will be offered bail is the classification of your crime, i.e., whether it is a misdemeanor or felony. When the crime that you've been arrested for is classified as a misdemeanor (minor wrongdoing, less serious than a felony) you may be in a good category. Also considered is your documented history of arrest or criminal activity and what type of citizen you are characterized as in society. The worse that you score in the areas of criminal history, status in society, and the seriousness of your offense, the more of a flight risk and danger to the public you are. The greater the danger or the flight risk, the more it will cost for you to post bail—if you are given bail at all. If you are not a citizen of the United States or an immigrant, you may find yourself ineligible for bail and placed on immigration hold until The Department of Homeland Security gives instructions to the local authorities. If you have strong ties to the community such as you have stable employment, family members that rely heavily on you, or ties to community organizations, etc. the likelihood of you running away or intentionally failing to appear in court appears minimal. Individuals who are exceptionally low flight risk are oftentimes released without having to provide any form of bail referred to as being released on one's own recognizance.

For those who must post bail, the amount may be reasonable or unreasonable in your opinion. You may be able to immediately provide the necessary cash, bond, or property collateral and be processed for release. The Prison Policy Initiative's 2020 report described the sad truth of over 555,000 individuals locked up who haven't been convicted or sentenced but will remain in jail until they go to court because they cannot financially afford to pay even the smallest bail amount. As a result, several states have passed or lobbied for laws to eliminate cash bails. For those of you who fail to post bail and must stay longer, keep reading. If your situation takes a greater turn for the worse—you may eventually get convicted and must serve jail time—this book will certainly be your secondary bible. In either case, every day that you are in the jail environment you will need to apply the wisdom of these pages.

Melonie Ware

Profile: Day Care Provider
Year of Arrest: 2005
Offense: Convicted for violently shaking a 9 yr. old baby to death.
Sentence: Life in prison.
Acquitted after the 2009 retrial when experts proved that the cause of the baby's death was complications of sickle cell anemia.

Siwatu-Salama Ra

Profile: Activist
Year of Arrest: 2017
Offense: Assault. While pregnant, attempted to protect herself and her 2-year-old daughter by pointing a licensed, unloaded gun at another parent who rammed her car after an argument.
Sentence: 2 years in prison.
Ra was compelled to give birth to her son in prison. Conviction was overturned by Michigan court of appeals in 2019.

Ju'zema Goldring

Profile: Aspiring Model
Year of Arrest: 2015
Offense: Jaywalking and felony cocaine trafficking. "..arrested for drug possession when police mistook sand from her stress ball for cocaine.
Sentence: Spent 6 months in jail because she could not post bail even after crime lab test confirmed that the powder in her purse was not narcotics.

Chapter 4: Fresh Meat And Recycled Meat

We have all heard the reference "Fresh Meat." Whether it is tagged to the new kid in the neighborhood, to new pledgee in the frat or sorority, or the new cutie on the job. In this case, you are one of the new inmates (male or female) in the jail. If you have been incarcerated before, then technically you are recycled meat. Recycled meat is old, preprocessed meat with additives (a worse attitude and arrest record than the last time) and preservatives (A mentality that says, "I've been through this before, I'll be fine. I know how to carry myself.") Nevertheless, until someone in the inmate population openly acknowledges you as recycled meat, you are unfamiliar and for now considered as "Fresh Meat." Note: This entire section applies to individuals in pre-trial detention and the prisons/jails which house the convicted.

In jail, authentic fresh meat is raw, not red inside, but usually green. In other words, you're a first-timer yet to be molded, mentally affected and infected, or uneducated on how to survive in the 'wild'. Kiss this book, my friend. Hope is in your hands, class is in session, and every passing minute, hour, and day you must be taking notes. You cannot stay green, i.e., gullible—you don't have a clue. All eyes are on you. It is your responsibility to get well seasoned (full of wisdom) and well done (tough) as quickly as possible.

You're Being Graded

Take many notes, keep your thinking cap on, and don't give your apples to anyone. You must understand that you are constantly being graded. Every good day and every difficult day that you experience in the eyes of your peers will be noted and recorded. They will be recorded both in your official institutional records as well as on your jailhouse resume. When does the grading start? Well, the grading started the moment that you were taken into custody. Let's consider the reports then we'll discuss the grades.

A file has been made with your name on it and with an assigned number that corresponds with your name. This file initially contains your arrest, bail status, and pending court cases for those individuals who are in pre-trial status. If you have already been tried and convicted, your file usually contains a printout of your criminal background (if you've had prior convictions or arrests), your current convictions, and your current sentence to be served. How you are viewed by the correctional officers during your stay in jail will depend on how you conduct yourself in their view and ears. On paper, they will keep a record of what institutional programs you participate in (such as institutional jobs, school, therapy, etc. and your record of attendance. Let's use a grade scale of G, S, and U—most institutions use a more detailed grading matrix, but the result is virtually the same. I have excluded a grade of E because there is no such thing as an excellent inmate. Every inmate will have to bend or break a rule at some point just to survive or cope. A grade of G means that you are a reliable inmate who participates or completes directives or assignments as required or even above what is required. A grade of S means that you do nothing more than what is asked and/or just enough to get by and keep supervising officials out of your face. You are not enthusiastic, but you accept that it is better to go with the flow than to buck against the system. Most inmates maintain this grade of S. A grade of U means that you display an anti-institutional attitude. You are a rebel. You refuse to do anything that will help maintain the jail, or in some cases, you refuse to help yourself by improving your skills, knowledge, or positive development. You are stubborn, bitter, and angry at the world. In your foolish heart you have made at least one of the following pledges:

"I ain't helping to make it easier to keep me locked up."

"I'm going to give them hell as long as I'm here!"

"I'm doing my time my way, not theirs."

As a result, you spend much of your time idle, which is mentally unhealthy, and forfeit the opportunity to have some of your time reduced. Yes, some jails shave days off of your sentence as an incentive for your participation in institutional jobs and programs. In addition to forfeiting the privilege of having your amount of time to serve reduced, many jails/prisons will issue you a citation/ticket often referred to as a notice of infraction. This is a notice that you have broken an institutional rule by refusing to comply with an officer's directive (direct order to do something), institutional work, or program assignment. The penalties can vary from losing some privilege to being immediately escorted to lock-up (solitary confinement).

Sometimes, the better your institutional record, the better off you will be when going before judges, institutional counselors, and even parole agents. Why am I saying sometimes? Well, unfortunately in many towns, many states, in the eyes of judges, parole agents, and the public opinion, no matter how good you are while you are incarcerated the reckless acts of your past will precede you. The stigma of having been caught for committing certain crimes oftentimes will cast real doubt on your sincerity and trustworthiness. We will elaborate on this truth later.

All Report Cards Have A Conduct Section

In your institutional record or report card is a section that indicates a record of your conduct. This section reflects your history of citations/tickets that you may have acquired while incarcerated. All jails have institutional rules. We know this. If you break the rules and get caught, just like in society, you will go through a hearing process to determine your guilt and applicable consequences. You may be physically arrested! Yes, this is a dichotomy. You can go to jail in jail. You may be placed in lock-up (segregation or isolation from other inmates) until your case is heard by a hearing officer. You will receive written notification of your alleged infraction. We will cover how to navigate institutional rules and correctional officers later. For now, just in case you go to jail or as they say, are 'sent up state' or 'doing Fed time,' you need to know how to navigate your peers in the Thunderdome.

Welcome To The Thunderdome

Jail or prison is a melting pot of misfits and casualties of misconduct. It is like the Thunderdome of the famous Mad Max movie full of scavengers, predators, opportunists, and prey. It is a hodgepodge of individuals from a diversity of backgrounds both good and evil. It does not generally exclude people based on color, creed, or economic background. You will find people from all levels of society from the poorest of the poor to the middle class and the wealthy. Do not believe the hype that rich (privileged) people don't go to jail. It truly depends on the person, their locale, and their specific situation. There are many people in jail who, based on their level of finances, are regarded as rich and hopefully will get the opportunity to enjoy their finances if they are released from prison. Certainly, there is a disproportionate number of low-income minority individuals incarcerated whose presence in jail oftentimes is nothing more than the result of engaging in criminal activities as a means of survival. Some commit crimes to merely cope and attempt to overcome their socio-economic challenges. Too many potentially good people have grown up in a culture, environment, or family system whose behaviors deviate from social norms. These settings are often referred to as dysfunctional because individuals within them tend to mimic bad conduct and inherit illegal practices as a norm. Yes, many people from those same communities either choose to be more compliant with the law or are blessed to experience interventions that help them navigate the gauntlet of temptations and never get arrested. Whether rich or poor, disadvantaged or lucky, the impact of the economic statuses of the individuals that overcrowd many jails can be debated to no end. Our primary concern is merely how will **you** cope, manage, and survive just in case you have a moment of overwhelming temptation or anger that takes you out of character and requires police intervention. Let's view a snapshot of the typical Thunderdome.

Enter The Thunderdome

We function in an open society decorated by billboards, and highways congested with cruising vehicles, busy restaurants, cheers of family outings, recreational and amusement parks, the sounds of happiness and play, and consumers enjoying the fruit of their labor, dressed in the ideals of liberty and democracy. Sprinkled throughout this open society is an insidious spirit that can randomly reveal itself in the heart of every person at some point in their lives. Everyone at some time or another has rebelled against the law of the land and/or its designated authorities. Because we can get totally out of character, totally lose our minds, blackout, and wake up to a scene of our victims and accusers, a secluded society has been established to protect the mainstream world from our spells of madness. It is populated by each of us who are unfortunate enough to get caught in our acts of defiance. This dreary world, I refer to as the Thunderdome, is composed of an array of over 3100 fortresses scattered throughout the country each muffling 120 decibels of clamoring residents and slamming cell doors.

Social, political, economic, and mental health challenges that contributed to major spikes in national crime rates were remedied by a wave of new jail and prison developments (the prison boom).

This drastically multiplied the national jail population from 280,000 inmates in 1970 to approximately 2.12 million by the year 2020. Many of those individuals —who dared to play Russian roulette with their freedom—felt the impact of their former lives imploding. They then transitioned into the dark side, into one of the many Thunderdomes. Even today, our gambling with temptations and using illegal methods to fulfill thrills, release anger, and instantly gratify our desires, continue to keep the Thunderdome populations thriving.

For every reader whose worst fear has already become a reality, your faults have already been televised and published on social media, your family bears your stain of shame on their faces, and you've already wobbled your shackled body off the bus and through the jail gateway. Welcome to the Thunderdome. Here the welcoming committee of correctional officers awaits your arrival and attendance in your first class, Humiliation 101. You have been excommunicated from society for a determined period that will hopefully instill a greater appreciation for living in a free society. You are no longer in Kansas, Dorothy. You cannot hear freedom ringing here and mama can't hear your cries—and she couldn't help if she did. Contrarily, you may hear a few cat calls from inmates who are already plotting to put a ring on your finger, and there are some big, bad poppas and mommas —as rapper/actor L.L. Cool J once said—that will knock you out! We will tell you how to manage all of this later. For now, let's get through the uniformed welcoming committee.

First, do your best to endure and get accustomed to performing a lazy striptease for the officers. Gradually remove every stitch of your clothing, underwear, and all. Don't strip too quickly or the officers may think that you are trying to get them to overlook something that you are hiding—like your pride. They won't be making it rain (throwing any dollar bills your way) but they will sound just as demanding, "Let me see the bottom of your feet. Lift up your arms. Run your fingers through your hair." Turn around so that they can see your bare derriere, drop down and squat as they do in the sexy videos, and cough (cough up a little more pride). "Turn back around and pull down your bottom lip, open your mouth wide, lift up your tongue" — you should feel a bit violated by now. Men, "lift up your scrotum" —the officers will have a more colorful choice of words, ladies, "drop it." Beware of demeaning, jerk officers who require you to lift or touch your private parts right before they ask you to pull down your bottom lip. Please, cleverly switch hands. Now that the officers are convinced that you are not smuggling contraband and you are feeling a bit demoralized, you have just experienced a profound exertion of their power. Now put on the provided garments and get ready to step into the ring.

In the left corner we have the defender, you, wearing homely prison garments. Nobody cares where you are from or how you got yourself in this mess. This spotlight was reserved for everyone that was silly enough to cross the ropes of the law, and who for some asinine reason assumed that jail or prison would never happen to them. Most of us fit this profile. Daily we watch television reporters who make a living from informing us of the freak accidents, tragedies, and misfortunes that befall the public without discrimination, and we never imagine hearing our names in the headlines. Well, this is the fight of your life, your number has been assigned and called. Look around the arena at the multitude of eyes witnessing your entrance and placing odds against you. These are not merely spectators, but also instigators; so, as you slowly walk from your corner, try not to appear intimidated, and pull up your trunks high and tight as we introduce the challenger.

In the right corner, the next corner, the other corner, and every dark, undiscovered inch of the building, stands everyone other than you. Did you not notice that the ropes to this ring were made of steel and barbed wire? That crowd that is usually outside of the ring cheering and jeering is now stuck inside of the ring with you and they are doing the same bobbing and weaving as you will be. Would you believe that some of them are innocent of the charges that have catapulted them into the Thunderdome? Unfortunately, someone didn't believe them, and others could have cared less. Now they are left to face the same burden as you, surviving in the Thunderdome.

For you, this is going to be a classic World Wrestling steel cage, battle royal. Everyone is against their neighbor, few benevolently team up, and usually, those who do help another are opportunists. They will body slam you the very first chance that they can get behind you. Alike old-school WWF wrestler Razor Ramon would declare "this place is oozing with machismo." Everyone wants to give the impression that they have courage or are tough, but they display it in different ways, which we will discuss later. As the defender of your humanity, your pride, and the sanctity of your body, be always prepared for a challenger to step up to prove themselves. Realistically, many inmates have no interest in opposing you or even talking to you, but everyone is impelled to acknowledge your presence. Why? Because no one actually knows you and since you are going to coexist with them in this dreadful realm, they need to know what to expect from you when the lights are both off and on.

Rod Blagojevich

Profile: Served 6 years as Governor of Illinois
Year of Arrest/conviction: 2009
Offense: Solicitation of bribes, attempted extortion, and wire fraud
Sentence: 14 years in prison. Released 6 years early after his sentence was commuted by President D. Trump in 2020.

Joseph D. Hudek IV

Profile: Son of a Delta Airlines employee
Year of Arrest/conviction: 2018
Offense: To help himself sleep during an overseas flight, ingested too many marijuana candies and experienced hallucinations and delusions during his flight and assaulted flight attendants and passengers.
Sentence: 2 years in prison, 3 years probation and $67,841 in restitution.

Chapter 5: Survival 101

As we mentioned earlier, the most crucial step for any person entering the prison environment is to **learn "who" is in your environment as quickly as possible and to force them to learn you as slowly as possible**. Wherever you are housed, often referred to as cell blocks or tiers, there is dysfunction in all the personalities that have become your new neighbors. The crazy, the strong, the weak, the timid, the intelligent, the clever, the foolish, the sociopaths, the perverts, the bipolar, the leaders, the followers, the nice, the nasty, the guilty, the innocent, and the informants are all mixed up together. None of them will have signs on their clothing or their doors to help you identify who or what they are. You have the great challenge of figuring out who is who, as quickly as possible, because the moment that you walk through the door, they are immediately working hard to figure out who you are.

In jail, everyone is an opportunist—and I do mean everyone. The most valuable asset to most inmates is their freedom and none of them here have it. Everyone is looking for an opportunity or resource to make their situation just a little bit more comfortable, or to give them just a taste of power or influence, even if just for a moment.

Earlier I mentioned that one of the key elements of the jail and prison environment is power and the second is control. Control starts with your ability to control yourself and your ability to control as much of how your environment affects you as possible. Acquiring power is determined by your ability to use and manipulate your levels of control for your benefit.

Perception, i.e., the way people view you, is the most important ingredient needed to establish and maintain a reasonable level of control. People in your surroundings in both prison and society may not clearly see or understand your methods of gaining control and maintaining control, but they most certainly can identify what they perceive as power. But power is the last thing to be concerned about, especially considering that few people can obtain it or manage it without attracting or creating drama. So, lets us focus on gaining some control based on how you are perceived. How your peers perceive you will determine how capable it is for you to progress with minimal incidents and how often you have seasons of peace in jail.

If your arrest is associated with a high-profile case, especially one that was covered by the media, your ability to control how people will perceive you is already compromised. Someone will recognize your face or your name and have already formed a preconception about you. If they have not already shared their preconception about you with their peers, they certainly will the moment that they see you. You will face the challenge of changing their perceptions to regain control. The moment that you walk into the jailhouse or prison you are on display. Everyone is watching you. Even the ones who are not looking directly at you. This is where perception begins.

The first gaze upon you is for general recognition. Everyone is looking for a familiar face. The face of a friend or the face of a foe. It is no coincidence that you are doing exactly the same thing but for somewhat different reasons. The last thing that you want, or need is to immediately see someone that either you cannot stand the sight of or someone that has a grudge against you.

It is okay to be a nobody, a virtually unknown, unrecognizable, low-profile case, with unknown affiliations. You will have total control of how you are perceived for now. Do not ruin it by looking scared and uncomfortable. If you have any acting skills, now is the time to use them. Fear has a pungent aroma that flows from your eyes and posture. All of the eyes observing you either discreetly or blatantly will see fear all over you if you don't mask it. Don't believe the hype. It is absolutely okay to be scared, intimidated, nervous, or uncomfortable considering that you are in jail where your life is in jeopardy every day, no matter who you are, or how tough you are. The key to maintaining control is to not allow your peers to perceive how you really feel inside. You must look confident and comfortable as if you have been incarcerated before.

Casually survey the faces that are checking you out by taking a casual glimpse. A glimpse not a stare. Do not stare and don't quickly look away. Your glimpse should appear as if you are simply scanning your surroundings for someone that you know -with a look of inquisitiveness. Do not make any awkward faces, and don't try to look brutish or intimidating. If you find this casual glimpse too difficult to risk messing up, don't do it. Just walk through expressionless and do not look at anyone. No one will know for sure if you are afraid or if you are a walking time bomb. Just know that they will continue watching, observing, and developing ways to test you until you give them some clue as to who you are and what you're about. For now, you are still in control.

But what if…? You're likely full of anxiety wondering about what can go wrong with the plan described. What if someone shouts out to you, or calls you a name, or does something like you've seen on television referring to you as fresh meat or proclaims that you belong to them? Well, you have two choices.

The first way to respond to the welcoming committee is to instantly display strength by casually (not threateningly) looking at the individuals who are jeering at you just for a moment and looking away. You want to give the impression that you are merely trying to take a quick snapshot of their face and move on. Why? Because these are faces that you want to remember. If they are that vocal in their efforts to get your attention, they generally represent the front line of troublemakers. They provide entertainment for their peers using the classic strategy of trying to force you to prematurely expose your personality, expose how sensitive you may be, and expose a vulnerability. You will see each of them again soon and you want to be aware of where they are and what they are doing, so if they intend to test you further, it won't be a pop quiz.

Your second option is to walk confidently ignoring them and try your best to remember voices to match with faces later. Again, look confident, not nervous, or irritated. Keep them guessing. Stay in control. In either scenario, although you don't visibly portray any sense of fear, neither response will free you from the possibility of being tested further. The other side of maintaining control of how people perceive you in jail and keeping them guessing is understanding that the curious inmates around you have nothing else better to do. They will continue pursuing ways to get answers to appease their curiosity. They are bored and you will be their new project until they find something else to do or someone else to marvel at.

I failed to mention that following the advice in scenario one to "casually take a visual snapshot of any individuals who choose to test you verbally" may accelerate how quickly you get tested further by them. This is because some silly people have complexes about people looking at them, some will perceive your mere casual glimpse at them as a challenge. It's displaced machismo. Machismo is from the Latin word macho and is often described as exaggerated manliness, male pride, male dominance, or the exaggerated need for a man to prove himself or be superior. Similarly, for women, it is called marianismo. So, stay alert. Someone may soon be asking you something like, "Do you have an eye problem? What's up? You were looking at me like there was a problem? Do I know you?" Keep reading. We will talk about how to handle this.

You Are The Most Vulnerable In Your Sleeping Quarters

Once you conclude your initial moment of being displayed and marched before all your jailhouse peers, you will be introduced to a new challenge. Dependent on what type of jail or what part of the jail that you are housed in will determine how you handle this next important challenge. You are most vulnerable in your sleeping quarters. If you are housed in a cell with a cellmate, be prayerful that they are levelheaded and genuinely amicable. They may introduce themselves to you and immediately offer welcoming help and advice to get you settled in, or they will barely acknowledge you. Stay in control. This is your most important first contact with a representative of the jail population. This first encounter can be good, bad, or ugly. This person, who you have to live with, can present themselves in many possible faces. Staying in control begins with not initiating any conversations but feel free to casually make eye contact. Allow your roommate to break the ice. They are analyzing you already because they are just as concerned about who they will be living with as you are. Several scenarios could occur. Your roommate can immediately begin ranting and marking their territory, they could kindly introduce themselves and begin to ask questions to get acquainted, or they could ignore you completely.

Let's look at the most uncomfortable situation first. Your roommate immediately begins to test you. Introducing themselves is not important to them. Their only interest is letting you know that you are in their house, they are in charge, and you better fearfully respect such. This is a tough test that many people handle differently. If you fail to look at them or respond they may think that you are afraid, and this pre-bullying session will be the first of many future occasions that will escalate into them disrespectfully invading your space.

Some people in your shoes are very aware that this is a defining moment that will be the headline of chapter one of your jailhouse reputation. If you don't set your roommate straight now all of the inmates around will also brand you as being soft. Not good. If you are good with communicating assertively in a few words, this is your moment to communicate to your roommate that you're going to respect their space and they are going to respect yours otherwise you both are going to have a real problem, real fast. Now, these are not textbook, foolproof words. Just an example. You have to be natural, but serious and communicate in a way that alerts them that you are not afraid to get physical if you need to. This roommate may not be aggressive but may just be exceptionally good at barking. If so, they will back off.

This roommate may be a genuine brute. If so, they will respond in a manner that shows that they respect your courage and back off or they will growl further and approach you to bite. If they go mad dog on you, I'm sorry but, you have no choice but to bite back hard. Just be encouraged by this—the objective is not really to win this first fight, though it would be great if you can— all you must do is fight back relentlessly and you will earn their respect. If they know that every time they bark and try to bite you that you are going to resist and fight tooth and nail, they will likely choose not to waste physical energy tussling with you. Oh, also... please don't get knocked out!

Don't worry about going to lock-up/solitary if the guards discover you fighting. This comes with the territory. You may need to make enough noise and curses to draw attention to your fight so that the guards can intervene before your roommate seriously hurts you or you seriously hurt them. If you are sent to solitary, cool. You get a time out from your nutball roommate, and you may not be returned to their cell once your time in confinement ends. The sour side of this scenario is that once solitary ends you will have to start the process of getting situated with a new roommate all over again. If you won the last fight or at least put up a good one, you should be okay because your reputation will precede you. Your next roommate will know about your spunk before you get to their room, and they probably won't bother you. If you lost miserably, you may get tested again by your new roommate and you will have an opportunity to redeem yourself. If you lost shamefully because you just can't fight.... Pray. You may be in for a very rough start. Be encouraged though, because how you finish is more important than how you start. Keep reading and you will learn how to compensate for your lack of fighting skills.

If you are spared the idiot roommate that barks and bites and you are simply assigned to a cell with a roommate that completely ignores you, you may be okay or simply getting a reprieve. If you are fortunate, this roommate is not very social and is not interested in engaging with you or anyone else. They want to be left alone and to ensure that they are left alone, they will take the lead by leaving you alone. This quiet roommate may genuinely be quite social, but they have a bit of wisdom that says, 'don't get too familiar too quickly.' They need time to figure out what type of character you are before considering engaging you in any real conversation. For all they know, you may be an idiot, bully, creep, psycho, or pervert. They are hoping to avoid an unnecessary confrontation too.

I saved for last, the roommate who "kindly introduces themselves and immediately begins to ask questions to get acquainted." This is the individual that most gullible, first-timers hope to get roomed with. These howdy greeters tend to ease your nerves just a bit after you have stepped out of the tense atmosphere outside of their welcoming cell. Unfortunately, this greeter that quickly engages you in conversation is oftentimes the most unsuspecting threat. When you are dealing with the territorial bully and the quiet guy, you at least have some inclination as to what you are dealing with; but not with 'Familiar Freddy' or 'Friendly Felicia'. Why are they so friendly? Are they just naturally afraid and as a security measure they immediately display their peaceful and kind nature to put you at ease? Hopefully, this is the case. Or are they insidiously trying to get you comfortable enough to let down your guards so that they can steal from you, get you robbed, feed information that you reveal about yourself to their crew that preys on new inmates; or even worse, they plan to assault you when you go to sleep. This is not to scare you. This is to alert you to this reality. So, if situations and decisions in your life get so outrageous or unjust and lead you to jail, these are real situations that you subject yourself to.

Deal with the get familiar, friendly roommate cautiously. Don't volunteer too much information but rather keep them talking by asking them questions. The more people talk the more they are inclined to provide more information than they intended to. They may give you some clues about their personality, habits, and motives. Don't waste questions. Ask important questions like, how long have they been at that jail, what happened to their last roommate, and what is the schedule for meals, showers, recreation, and laundry. You need to be knowledgeable of every moment that your cell door is scheduled to come open because in those brief moments you become accessible to everyone outside of your cell. Whatever you do, never ask another inmate about what they are locked up for! Oftentimes they will not tell you the truth and some people may get offended, defensive, or have such a complex that it instigates a conflict. Asking them about their offenses also opens the door for you to self-disclose your own offenses. Try your best not to tell anyone about your offenses. It's none of their business, especially since they will use your charge to make a preconception of what type of person you are, whether you are tough or soft, or whether your criminal case is associated with someone that they know or even love. None of these are good, especially not the last one. Remember, you are most vulnerable in your sleeping quarters.

The Dormitory Challenge

All jails are not exclusively constructed with cells for their inmates. Some do not have cells at all. Instead, they have dormitories or multi-housing units where several inmates are assigned beds and lockers in an open shared space or room. Mentally adjusting to this open setting is oftentimes more complicated for individuals who have never lived in similar settings such as in a college multi-resident dorm room or military barracks.

A dormitory setting, as expected, exposes you to multiple individuals at once that you must dwell and sleep around consistently. You have far less control over your accessibility, and you have no privacy. Dealing with one roommate and all their nature is hard enough. In a dorm, several people may be snoring, chattering, passing gas, hacking, sneezing, and not regularly grooming, i.e., stinking.

You Can Run..., But You Can't Hide

Beyond the drastically reduced possibility for a tiny bit of comfort in an uncomfortable environment, your level of safety is highly minimized in a dormitory setting. More eyes and ears have a clear view of you and any personal property that you possess. Multiple people can confront you at any time. You don't have the luxury of seeking sanctuary or relief in your cell. You must always be alert and on guard. In a dormitory, you can run (around the room), but you can't hide.

In these open living quarters, your first task is to keep as little personal property as necessary. The less you possess the less you will need to be concerned about someone eyeballing your property or having your property suddenly turn up missing. Understand that even the roughest and toughest individuals are subject to thieves. Very few individuals will confront a person that is known for or appears to be tough, so thieves usually will carefully plan how to steal with minimal risk of being detected. Let's nickname these culprits *tip-toe burglars*. Don't be offended or surprised by the possibility that you have to guard your simplest possessions like soap or socks. In jail, everyone officially lives below the poverty line. For the time that you are incarcerated, you'll generally find no one with a median income that exceeds $11,000 a year. If you are serving a prison sentence, at some point you may be offered or even required to participate in some forms of institutional employment; but your daily earnings will be pennies. A free individual earning minimum wage is rich compared to an inmate working just as hard in a controlled environment.

So, keep your valuables as secure as possible because almost everyone in jail is poor and desires to have more of anything that they deem valuable to them. Even individuals who appear to have plenty, possess only what they are permitted. In an instance or after an incident those who have plenty can suddenly have nothing and immediately desire to take your crumbs. Don't accumulate anything unnecessary. Focus on learning the personalities of the other prey and predators in the dorm with you. The quicker you learn about them, the quicker you can gain some sense of control over your well-being. You must establish a reasonable degree of control because you are never safe in jail.

Establish Your Own Schedule

You must establish your own schedule for how you will function in a dormitory. The best time to sleep may not be the time that officers turn off the lights. Observe and learn what kinds of activities are occurring at bedtime. Someone is habitually not sleeping. Why? Someone is never on their bunk at certain times. Why? Someone is on their bunks excessively watching, sleeping, or seemingly just relaxing. Why? Someone only uses the bathroom or showers at certain times. Why? Someone rarely leaves the dorm for recreation. Why? Someone rarely, if ever, eats the institutional food. Why? These are just a few of many things that you must quickly figure out on your own. On your own, I said! Don't ask anyone for the answers. You may alarm or offend them and instigate a potential conflict.

Whether you are in jail for a few hours, days, or months vs. any number of years, all of the aforementioned advisements apply.

The shorter your anticipated stay, the less time you have to assess your environment. Understand that if anyone detects that you're a short-timer you may become an immediate interest or target for those individuals looking to exploit someone. The less time you expect to be in jail the less sleep you should get. Staying alert is paramount so never fully adopt the strategy of trying to sleep your time away. You have too much to learn before you can comfortably use this strategy.

Don't Put Your Money Where Your Mouth Is

Studies continue to report that the median income levels of most incarcerated people before their arrest are nearly half of the income of non-incarcerated people of similar ages. But you may be one of the well-off individuals who was merely denied bail or for whatever reasons couldn't buy your way out of a conviction. The fact that you are far more financially stable than most of your jailhouse peers should be your best-kept secret for as long as possible. If you had a high-profile case or someone identifies you another way, you won't be able to keep your secret for long, if at all. Understand that you are now living amidst the physically and mentally impoverished who long to be connected to someone with the financial ability to make their jail time just a bit comfortable. Please don't think that boasting about how good life was for you at home, just to make interesting conversation or to gain favor or popularity, is a logical strategy to use in jail. You should never put your money where your mouth is, i.e., never talk about your money, your savings, your business, inheritance, or anything that indicates that you are a potential financial resource to some of your jailhouse peers who have been struggling all their lives.

Understand that you have been cast into an oppressed, depressed, and impoverished society where few are independent. Many incarcerated individuals were dependents at home. Some relied on either family members (in some form or another) or relied on government assistance for resources for financial support. You are a big, juicy, gazelle in a lion's den, and a bag of grain in a starving town. Anyone who can get close to you will want a piece of you. Some exploiters will plot and/or attempt to rob you repeatedly; some will offer you protection for a hefty fee, and some will orchestrate your robbery to convince you that you need to hire them for protection. Others will rob you and force you to pay them not to rob you again—Really! There are clever wise guys and gals that will, as they say, 'finesse you.' They will strategically befriend you by discretely feeding you positive jailhouse survival tips. Their mere presence around you may feel a bit comforting—by design. They will display a concern for your welfare, and it may appear that onlookers respect them. The wisest one does not have to be aggressive because they are so skillful with their techniques that you will voluntarily open up and share with them. You will find them favorable enough to reveal personal information or outside connections that they intend to use to improve their financial situation. As cool as they seem, understand that they want a piece of your pie. Realistically, if you did not have money and/or valuable resources, they would not even acknowledge you.

On a positive note, other than paying for security, your needs in jail are small. Your money will keep your belly full, and buy you whatever other pleasures are available, and you will maintain a few generic friends. As for your financial future (if your criminal case did not exhaust much of your wealth and you are at some point scheduled to return to society) hopefully will be reasonably intact when this is over. However, five things can spoil this hope. Bad or shyster advisors may cause you to make bad investments while you are incarcerated; leeches in the form of greedy family members suddenly have a series of financial emergencies; former business partners or collections agencies wage war against your bank accounts; you fall victim to some grand jailhouse extortion; the rivals of your jailhouse protectors fail at trying to lure you into their protection and they decide to kill you. I know it sounds extreme, but it happens. Lighten up. You may actually survive this jail time in one piece.

Meanwhile, spend your money in jail modestly so that as few people as possible know for sure that you are a meal ticket. Don't be stingy, nevertheless, towards inmates that you confirm to be mentally healthy but genuinely destitute. Sometimes there will be individuals that appreciate your gratuity and will become loyal comrades. They are in your midst, discreetly noticing you, yet paying no attention to you. They are struggling with little or no outside support, yet they will never complain because they have grown accustomed to being without. These destitute peers won't try to con you, befriend you, or petition for your sympathy like many panhandlers do. Oftentimes, they are too proud to beg. Never look for them because they will think that you have a deceitful hidden agenda. Simply examine the characteristics of everyone around you, recognize them, wait for a discrete opportunity to be a blessing to them, and be on your way.

Your money can help you when dealing with a guard as well. Despite their uniforms, correctional officers are human. Many of them do favors and receive favors. Befriending the right officer could prove to be a great investment for neutralizing some of the gorillas in your midst. Read more about the officers in chapter 7.

There Is No Place Like Home

Every person in jail has an innate desire to be among the free society, and they have their own classic "There's no place like home" stories. Some people take pleasure in sharing stories of the things that they did, and places that they went, and overdramatize their experiences for sheer entertainment. Others rarely, if ever, speak about their home life. Those who speak about, and share stories often use storytelling as a coping mechanism. Storytelling helps them stay hopeful or connected to their past identity. Others choose to suppress their sentimental longing for the past and their longing for freedom. They cope by placing out of their minds all of the things, people, and places that are now out of their sight. Being the storyteller may not always be the best coping mechanism because everyone doesn't want to be reminded about their good times. They do not want to be reminded of how long it may be before they can wake up and, once again, enjoy pleasures without restriction. Some do not want to be reminded that they will never return to society. Hearing the stories, plans, and expectations of others may cause them stress, cause them depression, and cause them to deflect their frustrations onto you. Additionally, never allow others to see or hear you stressing, whining, or crying about your being locked up or missing someone. For some, stressing over the intangible can be perceived as a weakness. Too much focus and emphasis on freedom, i.e., getting out of jail, is debilitating and can lead you into depression. Depression can lead to destructive thoughts. Thoughts of harming yourself or trying to harm others. Both can result in you being seriously injured, killed, or prosecuted again for harming another inmate. Reminisce about home, grieve, and cry in your own private space and private time so others will not misinterpret your need to vent and express natural human emotions as an opportunity to mess with you.

Duck Hunting

In 1949 Warner Brothers released a now Golden Collection Looney Tunes episode called Daffy Duck Hunt. Daffy was able to avoid being shot by the hunter, Porky Pig, by proactively removing the beads from Porky's shotgun shells. Porky executed his plan to hunt Daffy but was unable to add Daffy to his "bag" (hunting term) because Daffy was able to predict Porky's hunting strategy. We mentioned earlier that you are most vulnerable in your sleeping quarters, but there are a few other scenarios that we must highlight as a part of Survival 101.

There is always a possibility of facing a physical conflict in jail and many of them will not be instigated by you. Regardless of whether you anticipate the physical conflict or are blindsided, the best way to minimize your antagonist's ability to harm you is to avoid situations or settings where your visibility is obstructed, where your ability to elude your assailant is minimal, or where the officer's ability to see and respond is limited. When possible, never travel in the middle of a crowd during mass movements.

Crowds are classic settings for an attack because most assailants want to avoid being caught. Attacking in a moving crowd exploits the correctional officer's limited visibility and challenges the officer's ability to prove who undoubtedly committed the offense since everyone is moving.

Mass movements are those moments when a large cluster of inmates are directed to move simultaneously to places like the yard/gym, meals (Feed-up), school, religious ceremonies, etc. The more people that are around you when you travel with the crowd, the more difficult it is to see when or where your assailant may be coming for you. Many inmates have other individuals with whom they have established relationships and mutually agree to watch each other's backs overall, but especially during these vulnerable mass movements. They provide an extra pair of eyes and a shield for each other, but it is not foolproof.

Traveling on the outer layer of the crowds provides a safer ability to visibly monitor people's movements directly or with peripheral vision. Positioning yourself in the very front of the crowd requires you to use peripheral vision to detect sudden movement from your rear and creates space in front of you to easily avert and defend yourself against an attacker approaching from behind. Traveling in the back of the crowd provides the most comfortable visibility because everyone else is in front of you. An antagonist would have to turn, face and approach you directly. Without people behind you, there is good space to avert and defend yourself. Traveling on the outer edges of the crowd (left and right) provides space to maneuver opposite of the crowd but requires the use of peripheral vision to detect unusual or rapid movements approaching through the crowd.

Group activities create another potentially crowded gathering opportunity. As TV and movie dramas have depicted, the yard and gym areas are common places where fights and assaults occur. In these recreational settings, inmates are allowed to move freely about so monitoring movement is more complicated since movement is occurring in every direction. Individuals jogging, exercising, lifting weights, strolling around conversing, and conjugating in a cluster, create multiple distractions and make it difficult to see when or where an assailant may be about to strike. The ratio of correctional officers to inmates in these settings is small, so it is virtually impossible for the Co's to watch every inmate. They rely on camera visibility to look for unusual movements, but in most cases, the officer's efforts are reactive. Oftentimes the officers respond once a physical conflict has already begun or concluded. By then, it may be too late for you. In group settings, it is always wise to position yourself in a location that allows you the best visibility of the people around you. Hopefully, you have taken heed to the earlier advisement of learning about your environment and the people and personalities in it. Recognizing sudden movements is one aspect but learning how to recognize non-verbal gestures and traits is essential. Why? Because sometimes your attacker could be standing right in front of you for several minutes and if you don't recognize the odd or unusual, you will be easy bait.

Un-instigated attacks are the worst. This is when you are completely oblivious to the fact that you have become someone's target. Too many individuals in jail have been targeted because of their relationship or affiliation with someone outside of jail. When the enemy of your friends or relatives realizes your relationship connection, they may find some gratification in redirecting their vengeance towards you. If you are oblivious of the beef, you will never see it coming unless you detect something unusual. You very well may not be able to prevent the attack, but if you can sense the unusual, you may be able to either elude, defend, or minimize the damage that they can inflict. To help with recognizing unusual gestures and non-verbal signs of pending danger, after you complete reading this book, you may want to order a book on the subject matter of non-verbal communications.

Blind spots

Aside from blind spots created by clusters of bodies, every jail has structural blind spots, i.e., locations where the correctional officer's eyes and camera visibility are limited. Wise individuals who have spent a significant amount of time in a specific jail generally know where all the blind spots are. Blind spots are used to both pass contraband and commit assaults in a matter of seconds. As you learn the people in your environment, you must also learn the blind spots and be alert every time you are in proximity of one. The correctional officers are aware of all the blind spots and oftentimes they are attentive to monitoring people and movement in and around the blind spots. However, the officers again are subjected to reactively responding to incidents that occur after a blind spot has been exploited. Being aware and alert for yourself is your proactive responsibility.

To reiterate the need to always be aware of what is happening in the environment around you so that you do not create blind spots for yourself. Whether you are taking a shower, using a bathroom in an area outside of your cell, eating in the cafeteria, or sitting in a classroom your 'spidey senses' should be active and alert. Any time that you are outside of your cell, around other individuals, and 'lacking' sensitivity of who is and what is going on around you, you are momentarily blind and vulnerable. People who are studying you will recognize this moment and if they have a motive, they will take advantage of these moments.

Should Snitches Get Stitches?

The entire idea of snitching was historically born the first moment a person made the conscious decision that they were not going to suffer the consequences of someone else's actions. The topic of snitching has been of great controversy for generations yielding stigmas and labels such as "rat," "turncoat", "Op", and a list of more obscene names that we won't mention. Many individuals choose to exchange facts of criminal activities with law enforcement agents in return for lighter jail sentences or a complete get-out-of-jail card. In the underworld and corrupted minds, the act of snitching is regarded as a major violation, potentially with a penalty of exile or death. As a result, in jails and prisons are individuals willing to execute judgment on alleged snitches.

Many people have unfortunately been seriously assaulted and/or killed in jail by the hands of individuals that enforce consequences upon individuals labeled as snitches. The aggressor, oftentimes, is in some way related to the person who was snitched on or is merely a twisted jailhouse vigilante looking to boost their reputation by enforcing an obsolete code against snitching.

For those of you who are too young to understand what the obsolete code against snitching is, this is the philosophy. If you engage in a lifestyle of criminal activity, you are a magnet for consequences that, at some point, will attract repercussions and collateral damage. Everyone close to you may potentially be that collateral that gets damaged because of your actions. You knew this once you chose to engage in a criminal lifestyle or criminal activity. However, like most people, you were willing to gamble and planned to beat the odds and avoid getting caught. Because you made the conscious choice to play the game, and unfortunately lost, you must honor the fact that many other players played better and did not get caught. Karma (fate), in its natural order, will bring every other player into account in their time. To rob other players of their opportunity to beat Karma, by prematurely instigating their consequences can be fatal for you.

Why is addressing the issue of snitching an important topic? The most obvious reason is that the person who provided authorities with confidential information in hopes of making their situation easier may have been you. This topic may easily be a brief but of the most controversial of any section of this book because of the hard truth. Truth: "virtually anyone and everyone has the capability of snitching." From Adam snitching on Eve to Sammy snitching on Gotti to the kingpin snitching on other drug organizations—or their own organization, to the toughest, most ruthless person in the hood snitching on everybody to reduce their sentence, to the person who never thought that their life would turn upside down and find themselves facing a criminal judge.

Snitches are valuable assets in the fiber of law enforcement that both contribute to the maintenance of criminal activity and provide job security to officers, attorneys, judges, correctional officers, and any other position necessary to make the legal system work. In some major cities, one police officer can have a list of a few hundred of their own personal CI's (confidential informants). So, it is safe to assume that many other patrol officers and detectives have their private pool of CI's as well.

Earlier in this section, I referred to the code of not snitching as obsolete, because we now live in an age where the "Help Yourself Program" is no longer taboo, but a means to turn the worse situation into a simply bad situation. In jail, it is safe to assume that everyone has snitched in one form or another, maybe even you. No, snitching technically is still not condoned overtly which is why it's rare that anyone boldly admits that they have snitched on someone. If that is your story, follow the trend. Don't confide in anyone the fact that you provided officers information to either minimize your pending consequences, control damage that your actions have or may cause others that you care about, or for whatever reason that you saw fit to "help yourself."

Protective Custody: The Doo-Wop

The Doo-Wop may sound like a strange reference for protective custody. It was used in the early 1990s in some jails to refer to the fact that oftentimes individuals that were in the protective custody (PC) section of the jail were on PC for singing, or rather, snitching on someone about something. For those too young to remember, Doo-Wop is a popular 1950s style of music that highlight vocal groups making rhythms by using their voices to mix sounds and harmonic singing. Officially, protective custody is most often referred to by its abbreviation PC and is a section of the jail similar to solitary confinement but exclusively reserved for individuals who need to temporarily be isolated from the general population for their safety. There are some exceptions to the location of the PC unit. Jails managing overpopulation issues may utilize their segregation unit for both individuals being confined for disciplinary reasons and protective custody.

Individuals could be placed in PC status for several reasons. Popular celebrities can be placed on PC because they are oftentimes immediate targets for bullying and extortion since inmates tend to presume that the celebrity still has access to an abundance of money. Individuals that are incarcerated for taboo crimes like rape and child sex offenses may be placed in PC immediately upon arriving at a jail, especially if their cases were popularized in the media. If an inmate is assaulted or injured by an unknown assailant and/or the assailant(s) affiliations are deemed as highly violent, the inmate requires protective custody placement pending further investigation.

Protective custody is also voluntary. An inmate who is fearful of being hurt by another inmate and wants to make themselves inaccessible to their adversary can discretely warn officers that "I fear for my life..." This is referred to as 'checking-in to PC.' In a well-managed jail, officers will not hesitate to place the inmate on PC just as a precaution. Too often, crying for PC can be used as a tactic to be removed from the general population for other ulterior motives. For example, it is common for someone to steal property from another inmate and 'check-in' to PC to enjoy their spoils in private. An inmate can 'check-in' to PC on a spy mission to confirm whether another inmate is on PC hiding out from rivals. Certainly, individuals that enter a jail documented as informants in high profile cases or current inmate residents that suddenly feel compelled to inform about jailhouse activities can voluntarily check-in to the 'doo wop' as well.

It is important to note that going to PC voluntarily is stigmatized and will be a part of your jailhouse reputation either indefinitely or until you complete some extraordinary act of redemption that overshadows it. Of course, jailhouse reputation doesn't matter much to individuals that expect to be in jail for just a brief period; but, for those who may be required to stay a long time your reputation is like an aroma that will intrigue your peers or incite ridicule.

Alike every other jailhouse course of action described in this book, to check-in or not to check-in is a choice that you will have to wisely make based on your unique situation. It is called protective custody because it is to protect you from potential harm and provide a refuge for self-preservation. Whether by choice or by institutional mandate taking a detour is possible for anyone no matter how tough or timid.

Daniel Beckwitt

Profile: Millionaire Day Trader
Year of Arrest/conviction: 2019
Offense: Second-degree "depraved heart" murder and involuntary manslaughter (fire death of a man he hired to secretly help him dig tunnels for a nuclear bunker beneath his home).
Sentence: 9 years in prison

Mike Folmer

Profile: Served 4 terms as U.S. Senator for Pennsylvania
Year of Arrest/conviction: 2020
Offense: Possession of child pornography and criminal use of a communication facility.
Sentence: 364 to 728 days in prison. Served 1 year in prison and released on 8 years probation.

Chapter 6: Law and Order Special Victims

This chapter is one of the provocative and somewhat graphic chapters of this book, but it is one of the most essential chapters. Jokes and threats about people going to jail and getting sexually assaulted (raped) are commonly shared in most cultures. Teens joke about it, people refer to it to challenge the courage of others by saying things like, "If you were locked up you would be somebody's girlfriend." Police officers in interrogation rooms at times use the potential of an arrested suspect being raped in jail as a scare tactic. As a young teen, I remember officers from my neighborhood, making fun of a thirteen-year-old kid that they had arrested a day earlier. "Your boy is up in juvie. They're all up in his Hershey trail." Why such a fascination with the prospect of someone being sexually assaulted, especially a kid? The idea was both silly and scary when I was a kid but today, I have a greater understanding of the intent behind the thoughts, the threats, and the ridicule.

Violating another person's body, i.e., exerting your physical power in the most dehumanizing manner by invading their body creates a traumatic mental scar that cannot be erased. Some victims are mentally broken, that is, they no longer have any mental power to resist or defend themselves against aggressors. Some victims' self-esteem and identity are so shattered and tainted that they don't want to live with the stigma. They believe that every time they walk into a room everyone is looking at them with shame and/or ridicule. Ignoring this very profound topic would have been a disservice to everyone reading this book; especially those who may, unfortunately, witness the nightmare manifest into a real-life monster.

Jailhouse Rape Is Real

Jails are not populated by castrated men and women--- at least not in the United States. Seriously, they are not. Nor are they highly populated by people incarcerated for being sexual predators. Jails are filled with humans who still have the ability, and oftentimes the desire, for physical intimacy. Too many individuals in jail have been taught, before going to jail, that physical intimacy is an expression of real love. Many individuals in jail have been victims of sexual abuse in society. Some have either evolved into abusers themselves while others have retreated into being very submissive towards aggressors. Some individuals in jail have adopted the egregious viewpoint that sex is an expression of power.

The fact that prison rape has been and continues to be a major problem became more evident after the establishment of the

Prison Rape Elimination Act of 2003 (PREA). The Bureau of Justice Statistics has diligently collected records of inmates who have been sexually victimized. Regulations require all institutions housing adult or juvenile offenders to be audited every 3 years to ensure that the facilities are following national rape prevention standards. Four years after PREA's installment, according to the Bureau of Justice, 70,000 persons reported that they were victims of sexual abuse in prison.

PREA became a good act to raise awareness, but standards of how to discover, avert and address rape cases in prison were also needed. So, PREA was reinforced in 2012 with the National Standards to Prevent, Detect, and Respond to Prison Rape. Why? Because once people realized that they finally have mandated legal support and accountability, victims were far more comfortable stepping forward with their claims of being sexually victimized, so next steps and best practices in addressing the issue of prison rape became essential. According to the Bureau of Statistics (2018) reports of sexual victimization in 2011 nearly tripled by 2015.

Don't Drop The Soap

> ## FAMILY FEUD ROUND 1
>
> *We asked 100 Americans to name something they say to a person that they know who is going to jail.*
>
> **And the #1 answer is:**
>
> | DON'T DROP THE SOAP | 99 |
> |---|---|

For those unfamiliar with this statement, it refers to the reality that in many jails several inmates are required to shower at the same time with other inmates. Dropping your soap bar is a common occurrence. To pick up your soap, you would either bend over or kneel. Bending over or kneeling while naked in the shower, places you in a very compromising position. Bending, which I do not ever recommend, exposes your butt and/or vagina to easy viewing and access to everyone sharing the shower with you. If anyone has been plotting to catch you in a vulnerable state, this would be their opportunity to attempt very quickly to overpower you before you can rise back up. Considering that you rarely know what crimes every person in the shower with you has committed, there is always a chance that you are in the shower with an official sexual offender. Even if you are a sex offender, you may still look enticing to the next sex offender.

The implication is that someone is lurking or stalling in the shower waiting for you to drop the soap so that they can very quickly slide into your while you are the most exposed. Fortunately, this is not true in most cases. Most prison rapes are premeditated. In most cases, the person or persons intending to sexually assault you in the shower have been planning their attack. They will not wait for you to drop the soap. They will wait for what they believe is the moment that you are not expecting them, the moment that you are not prepared to defend yourself, and what they believe is the moment that they can complete the act and get away with it. Likely, they will be swift, threatening, and forceful. They prefer the soap to be lathered in your crevasses, not on the floor (no pun intended).

But let's go with the classic illustration and say you strangely do drop your soap; what about kneeling? Kneeling is the wisest option but still not safe. Kneeling allows you to maintain both a direct visual and a peripheral visual of many people around you. You can bounce back up much easier from a kneeling position. Kneeling does not expose your rear orifice(s) but does place your face and head at eye level with someone's genitals. With your head so low, it is easier for a culprit to strike you in the head or face, and grab you around the neck or head while another culprit attempts to force their genitals into your face. I know what you may be thinking. You may be thinking that your attackers may put themselves at risk of being bitten by you; but, if they have a weapon such as a shank (jailhouse knife) at your throat, you will have to make the biggest decision of your life in a matter of seconds. My best advice for you is this...when you are sharing the shower with others in jail, "Don't drop the soap!" If you happen to drop the soap ---PLEASE--- leave it on the floor and get out of the shower, even if you aren't finished washing up. I must reiterate that although "Don't drop the soap" is a famous joke, it is not a myth or an exaggerated illustration. Prison rape is very real and akin to the expression of power that motivates many sexual predators in the free society.

A biological truth is that jail does not separate an incarcerated individual from their natural desire to use their procreation tools. In jail, many people will still have the desire to be sexually stimulated and for heterosexual individuals, extended absence from the opposite sex may make them more inclined to seek fulfillment from their same-sex peers. In many heterosexual minds, they presume, "Hey, I'm in jail. No one will ever know." In jail, just like the outside of jail, some utilize sex for mere gratification, and others that use sex as an instrument of power, dominance, and humiliation.

In some societies, our sex organs are regarded as sacred hence the reference to "private parts". These parts of the body are generally covered, even when the rest of the body is bare. Some cultures, like those found in Islamic societies, require women to keep the majority of their bodies covered when in public, only exposing their eyes. Humans are reputed as being cursed with the "lust of the eye and lust of the flesh." Remember the story of Adam and Eve? Once they realized that they were naked, they covered themselves. Flesh that was once glorious and respected suddenly began to cause people's nostrils to flare, eyes to ogle, and heart rate to increase as their lustful imaginations become enchanted by an object of their desire.

Pleasure And Courtship

> *AND I'M FEELIN' MYSELF, JACK RABBIT*
> *FEELIN' MYSELF, BACK OFF, CAUSE I'M FEELIN'*
> *MYSELF, JACK OFF*
> *HEARD HE THINKS ABOUT ME WHEN HE*
> *WHACKS OFF*
> *WHACKS ON? WAX OFF... (Beyonce, 2014)*

Unlike a nun or a priest who willingly pledges a vow to suppress their fleshly desires, inmates are compelled to be celibate. Individuals in jail, who once upon a time, had healthy, regular sex lives, had to go cold turkey from sex once they were locked up. In the United States, prison institutions have a policy that both forbids masturbation and possessing any form of pornography. Yes, there is a standard rule in prisons that prohibits sexual activity including masturbation. The regulation in the legal codes for most state and federal correctional institutions look something like this:

(41) Sexual Activity: Sexual contact including, but not limited to, sexual intercourse, deviate sexual intercourse, kissing, fondling, or manipulation of the genitalia, buttocks, and breasts of another person, or oneself, in a manner that produces or is intended to produce sexual stimulation or gratification.

Understandably, masturbation is common in jail despite the rules. Most individuals are very discreet in taking the risk of getting relief before being discovered. Some quickly *masturbate* in the shower (so never step into a shower barefooted, men) while most others cover their cell windows for privacy. Note that it is also against the rules to block an officer's ability to see inside of your jail cell, yet many inmates will still do so to explore themselves in private during a time of day that they are least likely to be discovered. You will discover a few exhibitionists who cover their windows during times when they know there is a high chance of being caught by officers. These characters find pleasure when someone witnesses them gratifying themselves. They will ignore announcements, knocks, and any directives from officers to remove the cover from their doors. Any good officer would be compelled to open the door just to ensure that the individual is not harmed or experiencing a crisis. The upright officer would certainly prefer to open the cell and momentarily be offended by the naked exhibition than to risk finding a dead or maimed inmate later.

Lockup Love

> *WHEN I'M ALONE IN MY ROOM*
> *SOMETIMES I STARE AT THE WALL*
> *AND IN THE BACK OF MY MIND*
> *I HEAR MY CONSCIENCE CALL*
> *TELLING ME I NEED A GIRL WHO'S AS SWEET AS A*
> *DOVE*
> *FOR THE FIRST TIME IN MY LIFE, I SEE I NEED*
> *LOVE....*
> *(L.L. Cool J, 1987)*

While incarcerated, many lonely inmates yearn for consensual companionship, and some will successfully find it inside of the jail. Conjugal visits were popular once upon a time. Conjugal visits (extended family visits) in state prisons allowed eligible inmates to spend private time with their significant other, children, or other relatives. The formal intention of these visits was to promote maintaining strong family bonds and reduce the chance that a person would commit more crimes upon being released from jail and risk losing these relationships. Also, while incarcerated, inmates who receive conjugal visits tended to be more compliant and less violent which keeps them eligible for the conjugal visits. Yes, the conjugal visits allowed inmates to have sexual relations with their visiting partner... a great incentive to be on their best behavior. Currently, only New York, California, Connecticut, Mississippi, New Mexico, and Washington (6 states) allow extended family visits to inmates that meet an approved criterion. If you find yourself among the majority of remaining persons who are either not eligible for conjugal visits, are in one of the other 44 states, or who are in federal prison, you may resort to remedying your loneliness in-house.

Beyond masturbation is the reality that some will certainly have sex with others in jail for mere gratification. More often than some people will admit, many individuals who had never indulged in a same-sex relationship before being incarcerated will do so consensually. Why? Well, many people believe that love soothes a lonely heart. Jails are overwhelmed with lonely people. Some have been away from their significant others for weeks, months, and years. Some have never experienced real companionship. Some have never been able to capture the undivided attention of another person until they were in a controlled environment like a jail where people have no other choice but to see each other's faces every day, all day.

Courtship in jail occurs in the very same manner as it does outside of jail. One person finds something interesting or even attractive about another person and begins to strategize on how to get their attention and/or seduce them. It may be an inmate seeking the attention of another inmate, an inmate seeking the attention of a prison guard (correctional officer), or an officer seeking the attention of an inmate. Yes, I said it. Some prison guards have never experienced real companionship or maintained the undivided attention of a mate, or they are mentally fragile from a broken relationship, or they are just plain gullible. Pick one of these descriptions and you will find hundreds of them working in jails and prisons right now. We will come back to that later.

Consider these other factors:

- Jail is a place where many people reach the lowest points of their lives and in their fragile mental states, it is common for many to break every principle that they once held valuable. They shift from "I would never..." to "Don't judge me..." Some individuals simply stop caring about what others think and give in to their carnal lust.

- Some are seduced by openly gay inmates who sense their vulnerability like a stallion senses a mare in heat. Those openly gay inmates who dress or alter their appearance to look like their opposite gender (men looking like women or women looking like men) are usually skillful with seducing another person's eyes and engaging in sympathetic conversations designed to woo a distressed inmate.

- First-time experimenters, in some cases, have had a deeply hidden desire to indulge in a same-sex relationship and believe that jail is a safe place to explore secretly. Many of these experimenters, as well as others, will be released from jail and continue their normal lives as if their same-sex escapades never occurred.

We must highlight something important about the last example. When an individual "comes out of the closet" while in jail, then quickly runs back into the closet upon their release from jail, they are gambling with the possibility that no one will ever hear about their secret. I advise that anyone who is considering engaging in same-sex relations while they are in jail, should not do so if they are not willing to openly live as a gay or bisexual person outside of jail. There have been too many tragedies related to individuals who were released from jail and could not cope with the ramifications of their secret somehow being revealed to their family and peers. Jail is one big media center. There is a high probability that some inmate who was in jail with you, will at some point, see you in some capacity on the outside, or they discover that they share some mutual acquaintance with you. At your own risk, you may gamble with the possibility that your closet will have the hinges blown off. Some people, that you care about, may be disappointed or shocked as you stand there like R Kelly *Trapped In The Closet-Chapter 2* after being discovered in the closet, " ...I'm like "Whoa-o-o. There's a reason I'm in this closet."

Power

Power can be intoxicating and ruthless. Please don't deceive yourself into thinking that because you are, and have always been, heterosexual that you will never be subjected to a homosexual encounter or sexual assault. Many confident, tough, and straight individuals have been the victims of rape in prison by an individual or individuals who wanted to do nothing more than break them, humiliate them, and dominate them. Malicious individuals fixated on proving to themselves who is the toughest, or the baddest, or to prove some other sadistic point. Nobody cares how strong you are, how dangerous you think you are, or how great you are at defending yourself because incarcerated villains have nothing but time to sit back and strategize on how to catch you in your most vulnerable moment. Note: This is not exclusive to straight individuals. Openly gay and lesbian individuals in prison have a higher probability of being sexually assaulted because the assaulters have convinced themselves that just because you are of the LGBT community, you deserve to be raped or that you will be less resistant. Everyone has moments when they can be exploited. I repeat -- Everyone has moments when they can be exploited. Your job is to recognize these moments before your foes do, so you can disrupt their efforts. Spend some time studying yourself, your habits, and your patterns, and identify your blind moments. Recognize any locations in the jail where you could experience an altercation without the officers noticing immediately. Raising your level of alertness and awareness is mandatory for surviving in jail. You must be prepared for any of the variety of situations that you very well may experience or witness. At this point in this book, we are not focusing on your need to be prepared for potentially getting robbed, beaten up, or even stabbed. Yes, any of those misfortunes can happen; and you may prefer to experience being robbed, jumped by a gang, or even stabbed than to be sexually violated. If you are robbed, beaten up, or stabbed, you can replace what is taken, you can heal from battle wounds, and if you're not stabbed to death, you will have a greater appreciation for every breath that you breathe. However, if you are sexually assaulted, you will certainly heal externally; but the mental scars and traumatic symptoms may haunt you for the rest of your life and manifest in moments and in situations that you can't prepare for.

To violate a person physically is to hurt them at their very core. Afterward, the violator will always see their victim as being conquered and branded. They saw, they schemed, stealthy surprised, subdued, and stained their victim permanently. Jail is one of the worse places to be sexually assaulted because the entire population becomes aware of it and no matter what you try to do to cope or to reassemble your honor and pride, you will always be referred to as that person who was raped by "So-and-so." If you return to society, anyone that was in jail during the time of your incident, who happens to see you in society, either alone or with your family members, will recognize you. They may not remember your name, but they will certainly remember what happened to you. They may not speak to you, and if they do, they likely won't mention anything related to your incident; but there will be something about the way that they look at you, that makes it obvious to you, that they remember.

To Catch A Predator

Review... remember to learn who is who. Predators are not hard to recognize. Oftentimes they like to play with their food. They observe their intended meal first. They then put themselves in the same place or the same space so that they can observe closer and begin their game of familiarity. The predator will find a way to insert themselves into a conversation that you are having, or they may create a trivial way to strike up a conversation with you directly. A cleverer strategy is to invite you to join in on a group activity, sports game, game of cards, etc. They will make their invitation appear spontaneous and not premeditated. Their objective is to get you talking so they can gauge your personality and any other details that you unwittingly expose. The predator needs to size you up, i.e., guesstimate how easily or how difficult it will be to overpower you. The more you talk the more vulnerable you make yourself. If the conversation occurs in a competitive setting such as a card game or other tabletop games, or even sports talk, the predator will make statements to challenge your ego. They are evaluating your mental strength and weaknesses. They are trying to determine if you are passive, passive-aggressive, or assertive. You must recognize these tests and try your best not to hold your tongue when they make statements or ask inappropriate questions. You must say or do something to disarm them, flip their words back on them, or openly acknowledge that you are not cool with their style of communication. Choose your words wisely and make them few because this mental test could lead to a physical test. My best advice is, non-verbally display strength and leave them bewildered by looking them straight in the face, pausing for a second, and saying something like, "Enjoy the rest of your game." Yes, get out of the game. The longer you hang around and subject yourself to this mental test, the more comfortable the predator will feel. Abruptly exiting, with an unintimidated stare, may leave the predator wondering what to make of you and they may become cautious of you. They have no idea what you're thinking, planning, or considering. You will have forced them from offense to defense and hopefully cause them to re-evaluate hunting you. Just be on guard, because if you make them too nervous this mental test could lead to a physical test.

Stage two is the physical test. The physical test is not the actual physical assault. The physical test is a test of boundaries. A predator will create some scenario where they will invite themselves into your space by physically touching you to test both your strength and your reaction. They may playfully tug at you, grab hold of you, keep making physical contact with you during group sports, try to shake your hand all the time, bump into you at awkward moments, or put a friendly arm around you like they are harmlessly trying to be chummy. If you say nothing or do nothing to stop their advances, they will be motivated to escalate their efforts. You should not treat a physical test like a mental test. This is no longer a situation where you should abruptly exit with an unintimidated stare. This is a stand your ground moment and you should openly recognize and compel the predator to stop touching you.

These uncomfortable interactions are equivalent to what society categorizes as sexual harassment, and it is no different in jail. By failing to communicate a clear "No!" type response, the aggressor can misinterpret your reaction. They will deliriously convince themselves that you are being shy and that you are actually enjoying the attention. Ironically, it is a fair interpretation if you think about it. How do you respond when a person that you are interested in flirts with you? Depending on your personality, your response may vary, and the jailhouse predator is looking for any of these possible responses that are anything other than a bold rejection. Again, this is not a time to send mixed messages unless you are interested, and you don't want onlookers to know. But, if you have no interest in becoming intimately familiar or becoming this predator's prey, look at them the same way would look at a person that is about to steal from you and say whatever you would naturally say to persuade a person to stop touching you. If they are like most jerks, they will later test you again just to be sure, so be prepared to fend this predator off again just as clearly as you did before.

Will this guarantee that the conquest is over? Unfortunately, not. If you are unlucky, you may encounter a real-life sadistic predator that marks its victim and does not stop hunting until they are physically stopped. Keep a watchful eye on this person until you are convinced that they have accepted your initial rejections and have moved on to greener pastures. If, however, you notice that they are oftentimes observing you from a distance or weirdly showing up in your proximity be on guard and be prepared to fight for your dignity. This fight is worth going to solitary for.

Louis Kealoha

Profile: Honolulu Chief of Police 10 yrs.
Year of Arrest/conviction: 2019
Offense: Conspiracy to commit offenses against the United States, bank fraud (framed his relative with a crime to conceal his own fraud).
Sentence: 7 years in prison. Kealoha's wife, Katherine (former prosecutor) was sentenced to 13 years in prison for her role in these crimes.

Anibal Navarro

Profile: Former Correctional Officer
Year of Arrest/conviction: 2016
Offense: Conspiracy to distribute illegal narcotics, bribery concerning programs receiving federal funds. Smuggled drugs, cell phones, and other contraband into the prison.
Sentence: In 2022 sentenced to 37 months in prison.

Chapter 7: Welcome To Hollywood

Lights, camera, and action are words popular in the acting world and its movie-making capital, Hollywood. Where the big screens are saturated with individuals mastering the ability to pretend to be someone else so convincingly that spectators and audiences will pay to watch them. Jail similarly is saturated with individuals who have felt compelled to pretend to be someone else to survive, and they have provided a new aspect of reality tv that audiences pay a subscription to watch like *Lock-up*, *Lock Down*, and *60 Days In*. Those who live in these institutional environments can identify the variety of characters with the help of this chapter's descriptions.

Being able to identify each personality is crucial to navigating, interacting, or avoiding them, as necessary. From habitually pretending, some of the personalities that are adopted by individuals in jail oftentimes become their permanent alter egos. Observing many of the characters can be entertaining, hilarious, and even intimidating.

It is quite common for individuals in jail to see familiar faces, friends, or relatives who are also incarcerated. What often surprises them is discovering these familiar faces behaving strangely or participating in uncharacteristic activities. Baffled they wonder "What is wrong with them?" People who were once very lucid in communication and mobility can appear to be functioning slowly and even impaired mentally or physically. Persons who were always known to be quiet and reserved are at times the loudest and most obnoxious characters in the jail. Or the opposite, an outgoing, naturally assertive person seems unnaturally quiet, bashful, or broken. As I previously advised, an important key to maintaining some control over how the jail environment affects you is to learn both the environment and the people in it. So, let's meet some of the personalities and characters that frequent the jailhouse.

Fake Kirk

Kirk is a slang terminology, a verb that means to suddenly react in an angry fit, emotional outburst, or tantrum. Many people refer to this as kirking (kirking-out). A classic case is the volatile reaction of a person who catches their significant other flirting. Some kirk-out when they are denied entrance into a place where they believe that they should have been welcomed-- such as when they try to visit you in prison and are denied after their long commute. People kirk at parties when their money turns up missing. Intoxicated people who have less control over their emotions oftentimes kirk-out in the form of cursing, and brawling fits. A person kirking-out is a sure sign that a fight is about to ensue, and they seem to be welcoming the conflict. The start of a temperamental fit is a sign for you to get out of the way. If you are the potential Challenger of this hothead, there is a good chance that you do not want a physical confrontation. Physical conflicts are not physically healthy for you. Also, remember that one of your goals is to minimize your physical conflicts so that you may maintain favor in the eyes of the correctional officers.

Well, some people in the jailhouse have ingenuously mastered the art of Fake Kirking. They exploit the fact that most people do not want any unnecessary conflicts. They intentionally overreact and oftentimes they are overreacting to frivolous situations. They get loud quickly and boisterously challenge the other person. Cleverly, they establish their counterfeit, intimidating personae by targeting the passive and timid individuals in their environment. Their goal is to make a spectacle of someone that won't bark back, so they look for opportunities to instigate a conflict in some type of social setting. To initiate their spectacle, Fake Kirk may antagonize unsuspecting victims during card games, prison sports activities, and while eating meals. They may wait for the occurrence of some random incident e.g., someone accidentally bumping them. Fake Kirk may ask something of you or request something from you that they know you will deny. They may engage someone in a conversation that is certain to fuel a heated debate. Regardless of the scenario, Fake Kirk is going to kirk-out on an unsuspecting person that they believe will not physically oppose them. After a good series of kirking-out on a few passive victims, many onlookers will believe that Fake Kirk is a true threat. They will make their best attempts to avoid Fake Kirk. After all, that is Fake Kirk's motive. Fake Kirk will flare up, embarrass you, and threaten you, but one thing is for sure, Fake Kurt will not put their hands on you. Yes, I did note earlier that kirking usually leads to physical confrontations, but remember, we are talking about a Fake Kirk. The last thing Fake Kirk needs is for some passive or timid person to whip them in self-defense. That will ruin Fake Kirk's agenda and reputation and kirking will be ineffective for them in the future. Even worse, everyone that they previously kirked-out on may be inclined to take their revenge at the first opportunity.

So, Fake Kirk is careful not to actually fight anyone. Fake Kirk will flare up frequently sometimes they will flare up every other day. Their loud engagements will keep onlookers attentive eagerly waiting to see a fight. Attention: there will not be a fight. If Fake Kirk tests someone who unexpectedly responds aggressively, Fake Kirk will cleverly backpedal their way out of the range of fire without making it too obvious that they don't desire to fight. To avert the fight, they may maneuver themselves near a likely mediator whom they believe will intervene, or they may get loud enough to alert their allies whose mere presence may cause their opponent to back down (their allies likely don't want any trouble either). Fake Kirk may also position themselves in the line of sight or earshot of an officer. Why? Because correctional officers get paid to intervene in conflicts. "You're lucky the CO came," Fake Kirk may declare. Fake Kirk is a true phony.

Ironically, Fake Kirking works well for many people who master the technique. It creates a security shield that oftentimes wards off anyone that may be considering victimizing Fake Kirk. Fake Kirk gets to feel like a tough guy, especially as they graduate from making spectacles with cowards to ultimately fooling true tough guys into thinking twice about bringing trouble their way. Yes, a skillful Fake Kirk will challenge people who are known to be exceptional fighters and not pushovers. However, Fake Kirk is no dummy. If they have even an inkling of an idea that you are a dangerous vindictive person who won't rest until you retaliate physically, Fake Kirk likely will never bother you and will strategically attempt to befriend you instead.

Tip: When an aggressor is accosting you, using the tactic of Fake Kirking may be helpful, or you may end up having to prove whether you are the real deal or just faking.

Kung Fu Joe

Occasionally you will hear the grunts, shouts, and the sound of air being sliced. It's no peep show, it's Kung Fu Joe. Kung Fu Jo is in the jail gym, the yard, or the recreation area. Kung Fu Joe is meditating, kicking, spinning, and punching like a student in an ancient Chinese Tai Chi School. They are usually one of the calmer-spirited individuals, male or female who don't have to say much to gain favor and security. Their workout says it all, "Don't mess with me, sucka!"

The funny thing is that 90% of these animated Kung Fu Joe's don't know jack, i.e., they have no formal martial arts training, but their exhibition is good enough to fool most would-be antagonists. After all, how many people would randomly test Kung Fu Joe's skills? This would be a foolish risk to most people. Bruce Lee, Jet

Li, and any other skillful martial artist have educated us on how effectively martial arts can be used to dismantle opponents of all shapes and sizes. In jail, most people will avoid irritating or aggravating a Kung Fu Joe. Kung Fu Joe works hard to make their skills appear exceptionally good. Kung Fu Joe wants to appear as a fast, agile, powerful, lethal weapon to greatly minimize their chances of being involved in real physical conflicts.

There is always an exception to Kung Fu Joe's ability to find security in their display of skill and prowess. There is always someone who will get a kick out of kicking Kung Fu Joe's butt with a good sucker punch. Kung Fu Joe can't kick if he is knocked out. Even worse, a real skillful martial artist may exist among the incarcerated population and, rather than be a mentor to Kung Fu Joe, they may despise Kung Fu Joe's facade and expose them openly. In either case, when the cat is out of the bag Kung Fool Joe's reputation is ruined and they may find themselves facing more confrontations than ever before.

True story: There was a very temperamental six foot three 185 pounds of solid muscle Kung Fu Joe. He habitually used his training demonstration to blatantly intimidate people rather than as a humble deterrent. It worked until he tried to bully a gentleman who was five foot eight inches with a Napoleon complex. Napoleon noted that Kung Fu Joe never came out of his cell to walk to dinner. Napoleon cleverly waited for the cell doors to open for dinner, and ambushed Kung Fu Joe in Kung Fu Joe's cell while he was napping. Kung Fu Joe was caught by surprise, especially after realizing that his cell door had just locked them both in the cell, and he was unable to kick in such small quarters. Kung Fu Joe ate punches for 25 minutes until the door opened for men returning from dinner. Ever since that incident, everyone just called him plain old, Joe.

Shadow Ring King

There is an expression referred to as 'beating the daylights out of someone' which I suppose was to emphasize someone being beaten until they are only able to see stars and darkness. For those who are not familiar with shadowboxing, shadowboxing is when boxers demonstrate their punching techniques, style, and speed by sparring with an imaginary opponent. A shadow is always a safe opponent who will not swing back. Observing a shadow boxer can be intriguing when you imagine the damage that they would be inflicting if they were hitting a real person. Some displays are so impressive that most observers would be reluctant to face this stinging bee in any altercation.

Well, as usual, some guys in prison decided to capitalize on such an entertaining and intimidating exhibition. These shadow ring kings habitually make a routine effort to attract all of the eyes around them to bear witness to their punching annihilation of an Invisible Man. This Ring King may bob and weave a bit to display how difficult it would be to hit them. The fact that the Shadow Ring King's opponent is not real is the beauty of it all. As long as they fight something that doesn't fight back, they will never lose, and few onlookers will risk putting their reputation on the line to test the Shadow Ring King.

The opponent is invisible, the ring is invisible, and the winning title is invisible. True boxers, especially in jail, are reluctant to make a habit of openly displaying their skills. They understand that many viewers are potential future opponents or adversaries. An opponent who has been studying your technique may be less likely to be deterred from testing you, especially if they have identified a weakness in your fighting style. Some refer to such analyzing as 'sizing up a person.' It is the act of comparing your fighting abilities to those of a potential opponent who is unwisely exposing his strengths and weaknesses. Now let's be very clear... some shadow boxers are extremely confident in their abilities and have a track record to testify of their impressive boxing prowess. They could care less about who views their workout and they silently welcome anyone willing to leap.

So how can you effectively distinguish a Shadow Ring King from the real thing? It is not always easy. We know that the Shadow Ring King character truly does not want any trouble. They are banking on the possibility that a fine display will ward off all antagonists. Many of them can throw a barrage of punches through the air very well, but they lack the courage and ability to attack and defend themselves in the heat of a battle. Those who genuinely can't punch their way out of a paper bag will quickly get balled up when challenged by someone who is truly bad.

So, again, how do we distinguish the bad from the pitifully sad? Well, the classic rule is this. Those with real skills do not have to talk about it. Shadow Ring Kings often feel compelled to yap about their so-called boxing resume. They find it necessary to authenticate their façade by telling stories of who they beat up and how. Likely, they have never met or seen their victims because, as I described earlier, these victims are invisible. Real Fighters are usually much more reserved. Their reputation precedes and follows them and introduces their abilities like a ring announcer.

Even if they are virtually unknown in the region or the jail facility, you can sense their strong aura of confidence as opposed to an aroma of bull crap. The champion, Shadow Ring King, will certainly fool many people if they are also skillful at averting a real conflict. One defeat and 'the gig is over.'

Sho'nuff

There is no doubt that there exist a few characters that you should be greatly concerned about, unlike our previously described imposters. Some inmates have been poisoned by prison horror stories, before being incarcerated, and are pre-programmed with the notion that only the strong survive. As a result, some conclude that it is in their best interest to make a strong impression immediately and frequently. These daredevils aren't necessarily the greatest fighters, and they don't have to be. Their motive is to be a Sho'nuff threat. The fact that they breed conflicts is enough to shake up any environment. Sho'nuff will fight, sure enough, anyone and will never show fear. To Sho'nuff, every battle is a conquest to acquire more respect. Realistically, they don't gain the respect of their peers because their peers are merely intimidated by Sho'nuff's presence. His presence usually means that a wrong look or a wrong word with Sho'nuff will certainly instigate a physical conflict.

Sho'nuff is a drama King. He is always ready to rumble and will never be comfortable with feeling like he has lost a conflict, physically or morally. Relentlessly, Sho'nuff will pursue his adversary, so he is confident that his reputation as a true villain remains intact. Sho'nuff survives at the hunter because he dreads being hunted. Although Sho'nuff is always looking to demonstrate aggression, he will usually pick his battles wisely. Sho'nuff often will avoid individuals who are also loose cannons, who also will not cease in their eagerness to conquer. Sho'nuff is more interested in keeping his peers nervous, so if anyone is in their midst looking to exploit someone, in any manner, they will most likely bypass him.

The Sho'nuff characters are a greater danger to themselves than they are to others. No one is comfortable with a suicide bomber in their midst. No one knows who the next target will be, so as entertaining as it may be to watch Sho'nuff jump on someone, on any given day that someone could be you. Sho'nuff is referenced as a suicide bomber because he foolishly invites his demise. Many will realize that only death or maiming will stop Sho'nuff, and because he breeds so much anxiety, many are praying for his downfall and will eventually conspire to have the hunter hunted. So, in the end, Sho'nuff may gain the tough-guy reputation and gain plenty of victory notches on his belt, but none of that will outlive the story of how someone stopped them dead in their tracks. Running around accumulating enemies is sure enough stupid. Trying to deflect trouble by breeding trouble is counterproductive.

Demo a.k.a. Demolition Man

Demo is a sucker for pain who loves to fight just for recreation. Demolition Man fights to appease their fans. They will even fight officers to defend someone. Oftentimes they engage in foolish fights because Demo can be easily persuaded to fight over the most frivolous situations. Unlike Sho'nuff, Demolition Man does not go around antagonizing people to build and maintain their reputation. Demo fights because he is an innate brawler and realizes that many people appreciate good fighters and Demo yearns for the affirmation.

Demolition Man is noted as a good fighter, not merely because of skill, but because Demo is a people's champ, a rebel with a cause. He will physically fight for what he believes will benefit someone else or simply if he believes that he is doing someone some good. That arrogant, nuisance officer who everyone wishes that someone would punch out, Demo will drop with the 'one-hitter quitter.' If someone is suspected of stealing from within the inmate living areas Demo will help pursue the thief. If Sho'nuff is the new resident on the tier and he begins rousing up trouble, Demo will fight Sho'nuff every day till Sho'nuff gets out of the neighborhood. Demo will fight any bully that he finds preying on the weak. Demo's loyalty is often unconditional. Anyone that he becomes friends with can count on him to defend them, even when his friend's motives are wrong.

Although he is a brawling hero to many people, Demo is too often mixed up in situations that are sincerely none of his business. All heroes have a nemesis, and Demo always faces the possibility of meeting his match. Some inmates may find Demo's heroic antics to be a threat to their exploitive means of survival. Because Demo's behaviors are so predictable and able to manipulate, Demo can be easily lured into an unhealthy or even tragic conflict.

Certainly, Demo maintains many loyal supporters in the prison community, but none of them genuinely care about him.

Demo is often misguided in his intent and his behavior is also hindering his rehabilitation. While his fans are cheering him and amused by his every heroic effort, he disqualifies himself from being considered for early release. Demo's frequent incidents keep him in and out of solitary confinement which unfortunately is reflective of an individual who is a threat to public safety. While Demo is functioning as the jailhouse Avenger, he is unwittingly reinforcing the walls between himself and freedom.

Bull (Deebo)

They made many people cry in preschool, gave people wedgies in Middle School, and kept others ducking and dodging in high school. Those real-life versions of Nelson Munch (The Simpsons), Biff (Back to The Future), Viking Lofgren (Bad Boys [1983]), and Regina George (Mean Girls), in many instances, are right where most people expected they would be. They are in jail, still being a nuisance, and antagonizing the environment. Some of them have been referred to as 'the Gooch' (Different Strokes) but we will refer to this character by a more modern bully name, Deebo (Friday). Intimidation is their fuel and anything they can shake out of you is theirs to claim. In jail, Deebo is an even greater irritant because they are more difficult to elude in such compact confines. This Bull assesses their environment immediately upon their arrival, and with their glaring eyes, they mentally categorize the weak, the modest, the knuckleheads, and the strong. The true Deebo does not discriminate in who they will confront. Just as they will easily turn weak people upside down, they will bull rush the reputed strong individuals with even greater aggression to get what they want.

Deebo is a true bull. Do not be fooled by cows. Cows are individuals who portray to be bullies only to ward off potential adversaries. Cows will pick on people who lack aggression and who are easy victims. They fail to realize that no one respects anyone who preys on the weak and in time a true jailhouse bull will tread into the cow's path and there will be either mauling or mating happening.

Certainly, no one will fully respect the antics of a true Deebo either, but many will pretend to like them just to keep Deebo off of their backs and out of their faces. Usually, when you notice someone in various settings who is always being greeted by many people, they may be your popular socializers, or they may be a Deebo being pacified by peers. Deebo knows very well why he is popular. He knows that many inmates associate with him out of fear. The fearful use the classic tactic of keeping your enemies close. They try their best to anticipate when Deebo begins snarling like a bull so that they can get out of his path when he begins to charge. The problem is that this Bull can sense those who befriend him out of fear versus those who are merely acknowledging his presence. As a result, on the occasions when Deebo is venting his frustrations, his counterfeit fans may be his first targets.

Deebo is truly a menace that belongs in jail. Antagonizing the community appeases his craving to exert himself. Oftentimes this exertion is Deebo's remedy for coping with some feeling of inadequacy or some other complexity. Deebo's constant lashing out attracts attention and recognition which may be unpleasant to others but is gratifying to Deebo.

Homey

Amidst every jail population are individuals who are what we can call staples of the community. These recidivists spend most of their lives in prisons, and many will continue to do so. In jail, they are at home. Personalities like Homey too often had weak family ties if any ties at all. This is sometimes the result of not having spent enough quality time with their family members to build endearing relationships. Most of their family memories are from childhood and those memories usually are not good ones.

Homey is the epitome of being 'institutionalized.' Homey, being either a male or female, functions best in a controlled environment like a jail where responsibilities, expectations, and stresses are minimal in comparison to free citizens that bear multiple roles, responsibilities, and duties daily. It is easy living in jail when Homey still has all of their marbles. Homey is alike the wise Jedi Master Yoda. Homey is familiar with every personality in the jail, knows the dispositions of every officer, and can easily anticipate when situations will occur.

Sometimes Homey is not a Jedi Master, but rather a shell-shocked Wookie. Homey can sometimes have acute mental health issues; nevertheless, in jail, they are most comfortable and feel safe. Although they may not receive the best mental health care, Homey has fewer stressors to trigger their manic moments. A big reason for this is that most of their jailhouse peers are accustomed to Homey's behavior and allow Homey to be themselves.

Your task is to identify these jailhouse veterans that we call Homey. If they display characteristics of having Yoda wisdom, watch and learn from their interactions. They also will have connections to all the jail resources that may help make your stay less stressful. Remember to stay in control. Do not make your intention to befriend them apparent. When possible, try to casually frequent the same areas that they frequent. They will notice you and may eventually engage with you if they determine that associating with you is unhealthy.

CO

The title, Correctional Officer, is abbreviated as the initials CO. Correctional Officers can be the most complicated of all jailhouse personalities to understand initially because how they first present themselves to you may not reflect their true personality. They are sometimes the greatest actors of all the characters in the institution. Even stranger is the fact that COs can present the personality traits of every character that we have mentioned so far. They will Kirk-out, be bullies, hyper-sensitive-- Sho'nuff instigators, recreational brawlers, they'll practice martial arts moves on you, steal, lie, break institutional rules, and commit criminal acts right before your eyes.

This is not to proclaim or imply that all COs are bad, but they are human. They, like inmates, tend to adapt to the toxic environment by recreating themselves. How they present themselves in the jailhouse may be the total opposite of their personality when they are off duty in their personal environments. CO's greatest challenge is two-fold. Challenge number one is to not bring behaviors related to their personal issues to work and deflect those behaviors onto the inmates. This deflection can easily become habitual and shape the character that they choose to portray while at work. Challenge number two is to not allow issues and challenges that they face at work to go home with them and negatively impact their personal life and relationships with family and friends.

COs have an incredibly challenging job, and; not everyone is cut out to navigate this profession. COs are not exempt from the trauma that many inmates experience while incarcerated. They are very often witnesses to incidents that include trauma, psychotic episodes, destructive adult tantrums, major medical emergencies, and even jailhouse homicides. COs are oftentimes easy targets for inmates to vent their frustrations towards both verbally and physically. The question is, how does a CO adjust or adapt?

While some COs are disciplined enough not to compromise their true character and stand firm on their principles and correctional policies, many COs feel compelled to adapt to the challenging institutional culture by adopting an alter-ego. It is perfectly fine to be a CO who is sympathetic toward incarcerated individuals. Many COs have had friends or relatives serve time in jail, so this commonality may make them feel reluctant to display an image of being the hardnosed, by the book, enforcer. Many COs come from environments and communities that exposed them to little or no levels of intimidating and dangerous incidents. Some have no experience with being victimized. As a result, when they are rattled by an incident or aggressive inmate at work, rather than quitting their job for a more suitable profession, they may find themselves resorting to unorthodox or inappropriate remedies of coping. These remedies could include allowing themselves to be bullied and coerced by specific inmates to make it through the workday with minimal drama.

Some COs come from environments and experiences where they are familiar with drama, crime, violence, shady characters, and confrontation. They are not fazed by any of it and walk on the job already keen on the mentalities of many inmates. Their background, nevertheless, does not ensure that they will be perfect for the job though. Sometimes they are a perfect fit because some of them are highly skilled at walking the fine line of doing their jobs well enough to be respected by both their superiors and the inmates.

Geek

There are also your upstanding, by-the-book officers who pride themselves on being among the handful of officers with super integrity. Let's call them Geek. Geek knows all of the rules and policies and expects both inmates and fellow officers to govern themselves to the letter of the rules and policies. Geek will not cut you any slack. If they catch you wrong, they will hold you accountable. When their colleagues are acting improperly Geek's response may vary depending on the situation. An officer who is willing to receive advice or correction may receive both from Geek. Geek generally will go to extremes to distance themselves from unscrupulous co-workers. They try not to work in the same areas at the same time, if possible. Geeks are usually outcasts because bad officers can't trust Geek to cover their indiscretions. Most inmates hate it when Geek is working in their assigned area of the jail because Geek's very presence brings an expectation of uncompromising order. Things that inmates usually get away with when other officers are present definitely will not happen while Geek is working. Ironically, although many inmates complain about Geek being so strict, many inmates respect that Geek is consistent and they simply conform when Geek is present. Unlike some other COs, you know what to expect from Geek, day in and day out. Geek will always be geeking. *{geeking is defined in the urban dictionary as one who passionately engages in one or more things to extreme levels.}*

Jerk

Jerk is the CO who epitomizes their nickname. They are always acting like a jerk. It's them against the world. Jerk always has an attitude about something and habitually victimizes everyone around them to project their misery. Jerk is what they call extra. They simply do way too much to make a point or send a message. Jerk could care less about manners, doesn't care about anyone's feelings, and generally leaves people wondering, "what is wrong with them." Jerk is that officer who has fallen into the pattern of chronically bringing their personal frustrations and displeasures into the workplace. The inmates become the substitutes for all of the people that Jerk has a problem with. Recognize Jerk as soon as possible, be on guard, and try not to trigger them or make yourself a target of their antagonizing. You can be minding your business, keeping your nose clean and Jerk may say something to ridicule you or test your patience. Jerk's goal is to get a negative reaction out of you. They are looking for someone to play the role of the person that they have an issue with. Don't allow yourself to be baited by responding disrespectfully or challenging them unless you're feeling like Demo today and are willing to go all the way. Ringing Jerk's bell will gain you a lot of points in the respect column amongst your inmate peers and even a few officers, but the repercussions could result in a long time in the segregation unit or you could even be booked for assaulting an officer.

Be patient and stay out of Jerk's way as much as possible. Jerk is like the enforcer of his co-workers. Even though Jerk's fellow officers know that Jerk can go way overboard with their antics, many officers will turn a blind eye. They respect Jerk's 'go hard' attitude in a prison full of hardened criminals and other offenders who never imagined that their lives would take a turn for the worse.

In most instances, Jerk will unwittingly push the buttons of either an inmate who feels like they have nothing to lose or who has a psychotic episode and goes berserk on Jerk. Don't be surprised when you hear inmates cheering and relishing every moment. Again, the consequence for the inmate won't be very good. If Jerk doesn't experience fatal or career-ending injuries, they will complete their worker's compensation period and hopefully return to work humbled. On the other hand, Jerk understands that reputation is everything in prison, so they may return with something to prove and an even bigger chip on their shoulder.

Renee C. Johnson-Fritz

Profile: Patient Care Assistant
Year of Arrest/conviction: 2021
Offense: Solicitation to commit capital murder. Per a gang member's instructions, Johnson mailed a letter to a prison ordering the attempted murder of an inmate.
Sentence: 59 months in prison.

Shelby Buchanan

Profile: Day Care Worker
Year of Arrest/conviction: 2021
Offense: 2 counts of manslaughter. Distracted while driving and using a Chick-fil-A app; crashed into a minivan killing 2 young sisters.
Sentence: 60 days in county jail and 10 years probation.

Chapter 8: Gang Related

In the streets of society, there are groups of people that have bonded together because they share a common interest, experiences, and/or a common goal. Sometimes these shared experiences are trauma, poverty, abuse, abandonment, misguidance, and exploitation. Sometimes these unified individuals elect a common goal. They collectively choose to survive by unconventional means and mutually displace their hurt by inflicting fear, trauma, abuse, abandonment, misguidance, and exploitation onto others. 'Hurt people, hurt people.' Sometimes there are groups of people joined together not by any common traumatic experiences or environments, but they merely share a common goal that adversely affects others.

When a group is organized in their criminality, society has officially referenced them as 'gangs'. By default, many of us immediately envision a 'street gang' when we hear or think of the word gang. These gangs, however, can exist in all social classes, in all demographics, and all kinds of settings. There are gangs in communities, in workplaces, in schools, on college campuses, in the military, in political circles, on Wallstreet, in corporate settings, and even in law enforcement. Gangs exist among the poor, the middle class, and even the rich. Most states have statutes that broaden the spectrum of gangs such as Illinois Compiled Statutes (740 ILCS 147/10)

"Street gang" or "gang" or "organized gang" or "criminal street gang" means any combination, confederation, alliance, network, conspiracy, understanding, or other similar conjoining, in law or in fact, of 3 or more persons with an established hierarchy that, through its membership or through the agency of any member engages in a course or pattern of criminal activity."

The most interesting note in another section of this statute is that it is not necessary to show that any organized gang has a common name, nor does the group need to have any unique way of recognizing themselves or membership, or structure, or territory, or signals, or common beliefs, etc. The core requirement to legally classify a group as a gang is by providing a preponderance of evidence that the group **conspires** *(make secret plans jointly to commit an unlawful or harmful act)*, by law or in fact, to engage in a course or pattern of criminal activity.

Whether it is an overt, urban street gang or a secret gang of millionaires, the individuals in these gangs have one major factor in common, that is, their activities can be exposed, and they can go to jail. Many of them are already in jail and you are likely going to be exposed to gangs and gang activity if or when you stumble into a jailhouse.

In jail, you will no longer have the luxury of avoiding having to live in gang-populated communities, leaving the neighborhood at will, leaving jobs, or social circles dominated by gang influences. In jail, you do not have the convenience of easily escaping, avoiding, or being oblivious to the existence of gangs. While in jail, you are more accessible and vulnerable to gangs because both you and the gangs are confined to the same dwelling space.

In jail, there are two classes of people—gang members and non-gang members. How you function in jail, cope with jail, establish a degree of safety in jail, socialize in jail, or even survive in jail depends on which class you are in. If you are not already a member of a gang, you will have many opportunities or moments where you may feel the need to join a gang, or you may be compelled to join a gang. It all depends on who you are deep down on the inside. Many people choose to join a gang while in jail, while others are determined not to align themselves with gang members no matter what.

Should You Join a Gang?

If you have the misfortune of being detained or sentenced to a jail that has a lot of gang activity, once you follow Chapter 4's advisement "Learn who is who, before they learn you", a decision has to be made. Take a long hard look in the mirror, be honest with yourself, and 'determine who you have the ability to be.' I did not say 'determine who you are' because in jail you are in survival mode 24/7. Realistically, you may assess your environment, the activity in it, and the personalities that coexist with you and determine that you need to become someone else to survive.

If you are already walking into the jailhouse as a gang member, you may not have a choice but to communicate your gang affiliation as soon as possible. Sometimes, you won't need to announce yourself because someone familiar with your gang affiliation will recognize you and spread the news before you openly acknowledge it. You may be one of many individuals who reluctantly joined a gang in society, for whatever reason, and now you hope to have a break from the gang demands while you are in jail. Your plan may be to resist exposing your affiliation and hope to fly under the radar while you are inside. Sorry to burst your bubble; but you are 'between a rock and a hard place.' There is a good chance that someone is going to figure out your affiliation at some point. It can be revealed by a correctional officer who found out from your case file, or you may have a recognizable tattoo, or some inmates that are studying you will do their research and 'the cat will be out of the bag.' What happens next is unpredictable.

Other members of your gang may feel slighted or betrayed by your attempt to go AWOL. They will certainly approach you in some way, and you best be ready with a reasonable explanation that makes sense to them—that is assuming that they approach you intending to talk at all. Depending on the personality of the individual running the gang inside of the jail, you can either be harmed to set an example for others, or you may be sanctioned with another penalty, fine, or debt to repay for your act of disloyalty. Not revealing your gang affiliation is a gamble. You have to determine if you can handle the consequences of being recognized or being discovered after an undetermined number of hours or days. Unfortunately, there is an exceptionally good chance that you will be discovered at some point.

There surprisingly is some benefit to being a member of a gang in jail. You automatically gain a level of protection and access to whatever resources that the gang has already established. How strong this level of protection is will depend on how strong and influential your gang is in this particular jail. I reiterate 'this particular jail' because a gang that is strong in one jail may be weak in another jail based on two classic principles, "There is strength in numbers" and "the body is only as strong as the head." If your gang has a large presence in the jail, there is a good chance that the gang has a lot of power and/or influence.

For clarification, power and influence are not synonymous. Power in jail is the ability to make people do things for you on-demand, for your benefit, or for your pleasure, but it is predominantly fueled by other people's fear. Power, therefore, makes people do things for you. Power compels people to please you out of fear of being harmed and by acknowledging your ability to make jail life more miserable for them. This fear ensures that power is always self-destructive. People are tormented by fear, so no matter how cooperative people are, they are always praying for your downfall. When the adverse power structure falls, people can be relieved of their anxiety, and they can better manage their jail time without the cloud of fear that some gang leaders and gangs feed off. Take note that power is always overrun when someone bigger and badder, or wiser steps into the environment and figures out a way to poison the power structure with dissension or defeat it in all-out combat.

Contrarily, influence is the ability to inspire people to do things for you even when you don't ask them to. Influence is fueled by a quality that makes people trust and feel genuinely safe engaging with you. This quality is humility. It is unselfish and considerate, so it causes people to be fond of you rather than fearful of you. Influential people or influential gangs in prison can acquire favor with the jail officers and jail administrators. As a result, this influence produces positive change that transcends the gang. Also, influence inherits power. This version of power still causes people to do things for you to please you and it is still associated with fear. This fear, however, is not driven by people's fear of your ability to inflict harm or misery, but by their fear of you losing your influence. When a gang has influence it can be empowered by keeping a reasonable degree of safety and peace in the jail atmosphere. This is unadulterated power that can coexist with influence.

So, please note, that a gang of substantial numbers doesn't guarantee power. A smaller gang can have more power and influence than a larger gang. How? It all depends on who is running the gang. Your gang can be large and have a leader that lacks wisdom, maturity, and strong connections with the correctional officers and networks outside of the jail. When you have a leader that lacks these qualities and vision, the people under them will perish and struggle to benefit from their numbers.

Try not to misinterpret the description of prison gangs as any advocacy of prison gangs. You and you alone will have to choose what survival strategies you need to follow to manage and cope with being incarcerated. You don't have to be affiliated with a gang to be safe and/or manage with minimal drama, but you do have to be attentive to who the gang members are and how their activities can potentially impact you directly or indirectly. Learn who is who and distinguish which gangs are run by power or influence. Some gangs attract and recruit members through their promotion of brotherhood/sisterhood. Many individuals that have little to no reliable outside support find a sense of comfort in the camaraderie afforded to them by these gangs. There is always a tradeoff though and the biggest and most valuable element of this brotherhood/sisterhood is loyalty. You will be bound by loyalty, and loyalty to a gang can have you wallowing in jailhouse pleasures today and bleeding tomorrow.

Dwayne Stafford

Profile: Public-made Hero
Year of Arrest/conviction: 2015
Offense: Strong armed robbery; first degree assault and battery.
Sentence: Unable to post $100,000 bond and remained in jail for 1 year and 5 months without a trial. Bail finally paid by public donations after Stafford"s cell door was left unsecured and he beat up mass murder Dylaan Roof while Roof was taking a shower.

Chapter 9: Is It Jailhouse Religion?

Yes, we are going to wrap up this edition of this self-help, road map, textbook slash survival kit by addressing another controversial topic of religion in prison. Religion is allowed to be practiced in virtually every jail/prison, specifically in the United States. By way of both The First Amendment protections of a prisoner's right to practice his or her choice of religion and the Religious Land Use and Institutionalized Persons Act of 2000 (RLUIPA), the right to exercise religious beliefs is afforded in all penal institutions. Many individuals who enter jail already actively identify with a specific religion or faith, or they have identified with one or more religious groups in their past.

As in many instances where a new law is implemented, there are always instances of resistance to change by some agencies or individuals responsible for updating and enforcing policies in respect of the new law. Each institution has assigned Chaplains who are charged with ensuring the Constitutional religious rights of the inmates through providing pastoral care, religious worship services, religious studies, and contracting other spiritual leaders and volunteers to supplement serving the diversity of religions practiced by inmates. Unfortunately, many chaplains don't have a level of influence with the officials and officers of their assigned institutions to ensure that the religious rights of inmates are consistently honored to the letter of the law. Presumably, because the majority of chaplains in prisons are Protestant Christians, approximately 84% in federal prisons, there have often been implications of bias in the quality of services and resources afforded to non-Christian inmates. This lack of faith diversity among the chaplaincy staff was highlighted in The Office of the Inspector General's 2020 audit of the Federal Bureau of Prisons' oversight of its Chaplaincy Services Program. The underrepresentation of the other 20-plus common religious groups was deemed unsafe and ineffective.

Being considerate, chaplains are the sole individuals in an essential role that has been experiencing staffing shortages, so they rely on volunteers to provide religious service support. However, the OIG audit noted that in their Chaplain Services Resources analysis that there were 2,911 total volunteers to serve the Protestant Christian, Church of Christ, Jehovah's Witness, and Catholic inmate faith groups compared to 242 volunteers to serve the Jewish, Hindu, Buddhist, Muslim, Nation of Islam and American Indian inmate faith groups. At first glance of the numbers, a critic's defense would likely be that the staffing and resources should be in proportion to the number of inmates that are members of each faith group, especially considering that chaplains surveyed stated that Christians make up approximately two-thirds of the inmate population. This argument would be the same as agreeing that it is okay for a country to provide most and best resources to whichever ethnic group is the largest which is clearly discrimination.

This is why the OIG, after also recognizing that the inmate faith groups are far more diverse now than when the chaplains were surveyed in 2011, described that the staffing deficits created safety risk. Those risks were primarily described as chaplains having to rely on select inmates to lead religious services who were poorly monitored and prone to establish power and influence within the population. As we described in Chapter 5, few people can obtain power or manage it without attracting or creating drama. Also, consider that the primary goal for all inmates in jail is to survive and part of surviving is ensuring that your physiological and safety needs are met before anything else. If another religious group appears to have a greater level of support and far more resources many inmates initiate what chaplains refer to as 'switching' or moving from one faith group to another. In an environment where social groups become like family and sensitivity to loyalty is extreme, switching is not highly favored and can instigate conflicts.

If the end game of incarcerating an individual is to rehabilitate them—or habilitate some—and participating in faith-based programs in jail have in recent studies shown to improve prosocial behavior through innovative and holistic methods, anyone incarcerated should be drawn to the religious group of their choice and receive equitable supports and spiritual benefits.

So, it should be absolutely understandable that there exists a classic phenomenon that after an individual's life has taken a hard left turn and they wake up behind bars, they feel compelled to call on a higher power. Whether they are cursing and screaming at God, "Whyyyyyyyyy!" or crying out to God, "Please help me," or in repentance declaring, "Lord, if you get me out of this one... I promise..." their God's phone is ringing off of the hook.

Too often, the practice of religion in jail is undervalued and referred to as Jailhouse religion. This is oftentimes the result of people who are not only highly disappointed by the fact that you have gone to jail, but they are oftentimes irate by the fact that you dare to wait until you are behind bars to acquire the spiritual insight that may have kept you out of jail in the first place. Your affiliation or sudden desire to take religion seriously may appear as a façade to many people, especially since so many people have gone to jail and professed their rejuvenated faith as a means of manipulating authorities and relatives.

Other individuals that are close to you will praise the possibility that your life's turn for the worse may have been a catalyst to opening your heart to receive the spiritual wisdom that can change your life for the better long-term. Many people will attest that it was not until they were in jail where they had an extremely limited number of recreational activities, had very few worldly distractions, and had an overwhelming amount of private time to reflect on their life that they considered taking religion seriously. Yet, the stigma associated with religion, or a faith-guided lifestyle that is acquired in jail is perpetuated. Even 73% of state chaplains surveyed by the Pew Research Center proclaimed that "religious-based programs are absolutely critical to an incarcerated person's successful rehabilitation."

Do not be concerned about what others think if you choose to pursue affiliating, practicing, or whole-heartedly adopting a lifestyle shaped by a religion of your choice while you are incarcerated. Religious groups in prison are in most cases a far safer group to affiliate yourself with rather than joining a gang or adopting an alter-ego to endure daily jailhouse stressors. The key is, to be honest with yourself about your motives. There are clusters of individuals in prisons that bond together and support each other merely because they have respect for and exercise the same faith. You will recognize this as you observe and learn who is who. If you join a religious group merely to give the appearance that somebody has your back for protection or only for the resources that are provided to and shared amongst the religious groups, you won't fool everyone for long. Remember, as you are studying the people in your environment, the people in your environment are studying you. If your charade is discovered, you won't be harshly penalized as you would if you were in a gang, but it will change the way many in the group interact with and treat you. A positive note is that many religious groups share the universal belief that we are all a work in progress. Some of them endorse the phenomenon that if a person fakes long enough, they can eventually become authentic. So, do not get indignant when you recognize that people in your religious circle are treating you a bit differently. If you were honest with yourself, you knew that you had an ulterior motive for initially joining the group but there is time for redemption. Do not be overconcerned with what they think now or your relatives back at home. Focus on genuinely learning and understanding the life principles of whichever religion you adopt and in time people will recognize the real deal as quickly as they recognize fakers.

Be encouraged because there is no such thing as the reputed jailhouse religion. There are religions of many types that exist virtually everywhere on earth, both outside and inside jail walls. Theoretically, there are far more people in the free society that profess religion but exercise lifestyles, attitudes, and motives totally opposite of their doctrine than their incarcerated religious counterparts. Truthfully, there exists an abundance of people who developed a strong spiritual faith while in jail, positively transformed their lives from their worse conditions to becoming upstanding citizens, are highly blessed in their endeavors and have never returned to jail.

There are certainly advantages to being disciplined with your religion while in prison. Inmates tend to have a higher level of respect for individuals who consistently display that they are genuine examples of their religious beliefs. They recognize your routine of attending worship or study classes, independent studying, prayer, your style of communication, and your temperament. Remember... in jail everyone is nosey as a part of their strategy of self-preservation. Initially, they spend much time observing and looking for inconsistencies. Why? The simple answer is that many people have trust issues, especially in jail, and rightfully so. People have also been conditioned to frown upon individuals that adorn the cloak of religious piety only to prove themselves unworthy. Jails are full of people whose lives have taken such a bad turn that the only thing they have left to keep them wanting to breathe is their faith in God. They are encouraged and hopeful when their faith is reinforced by strong examples of others that seem to be blessed for their faithfulness, despite being incarcerated. Some are discouraged, confused, and offended by any mockery of their lifeline.

In summary, staying actively engaged in available religious services and activities while incarcerated has exceptional benefits. Thousands of volunteers and chaplains representing real faith groups have dedicated themselves to being a mental buffer to populations of men and women who can only overcome the crippling effects of the prison environment and experience with a dedicated lifeline of hope that teaches transformational spiritual principles. Many prisons, especially some of the reputed most violent "failed state" institutions, have recognized the essence of prison ministry and have begun to favor faith-based organizations as the priority drivers of their rehabilitative programs. The most effective prison ministries practice a holistic methodology that invests not only in helping inmates establish the mental fortitude required to endure the jail chaos, heal from traumas, and develop a strong spiritual foundation; but they also help inmates reinforce and restore relationships with family members, motivate them to enhance their skillsets, and instill a new level of respect for their communities through restorative justice approaches. Acquiring spiritual wisdom that improves the way that you make decisions and improves your overall lifestyle can fortify your mental and physical health. Overcoming the shame and trauma of who you were, what you did, or what you were accused of doing can be achieved with help of change agents within the religious organization of your preference who will shift your focus to who you can be and will be. Being disciplined with your faith walk while incarcerated can put you at less risk of being victimized, can minimize potential altercations, and can gain you a safer support system that will make jail life a bit easier. Nothing is foolproof though. There will be characters in jail that are so cold-hearted, jaded, and even mentally impaired that your religion means absolutely nothing to them. You can fill your heart with the faith of your religion, but while in jail you are still subjected to living among people who are all trying to cope with managing the worst season of their lives. Spiritual wisdom --and this book-- can help you navigate through the chaos, but there are no guarantees that you will remain unscathed, trauma-free, and not a become casualty throughout your season of adversity in jail. Nevertheless, the covering of strong, consistent faith and a like-minded brotherhood or sisterhood can provide support and promote a genuine level of self-discipline that can transcend prison walls.

Alfred Chesnut, Andrew Stewart & Ransom Watkins

Profile: 16-Year old Black Students
Year of Arrest: 1984
Offense: Murder
Sentence: Life in Prison
Convicted of Murdering a 14-year old for an NBA Jacket. Exonerated after serving 36 years in prison due to "police and prosecutorial misconduct" to include "coaching and coercion of other teenage witnesses to make their case.

Summation: Time Waits For No-one

With every second, time moves forward and farther into the future with no regard for our preferences, and time has no respect for where you are at this present point in life. Every moment spent incarcerated is irreplaceable. In the free world, all the friends, relatives, siblings, children, nieces, nephews, and grandchildren continue to grow and develop and share life experiences while their incarcerated loved one is absent and oftentimes 'out of sight, out of mind.' While the incarcerated person's social role, influence, and presence in society are on pause, time keeps moving forward. In one turn, every role, responsibility, and expectation that everyone relied on from you will be replaced, substituted, or deleted from their lifestyles. They will naturally move forward despite your absence and create new memories without your physical existence. Regardless of why or how you wound up in jail, right now your job is to survive, overcome, and redeem your self-worth. Despite how devalued, you may sometimes feel, you can resiliently recreate yourself. You cannot go back in time and undo the circumstances that catapulted you into jail, nor change what many people think of you, but you can change how **you** feel about that person looking back at you in the mirror. Even if your offenses dictated that you have indefinitely forfeited an opportunity to return to society, through engaging in positive activities, literature, and programs you will gain wisdom and learn how to positively impact the lives of individuals beyond your physical reach. Learning how to survive while incarcerated can translate into saving and changing lives!

Acknowledgments

A strong group of supporters and followers are intrigued by how resilient and productive I have been despite my plight. Most people have no idea that this intellectual and genteel, professional had once been led astray and seemed lost in a wilderness for years, only surviving by God's grace. Inside my 'belly of a whale' experience, I accepted the call of alerting and enlightening others who may take for granted the potentially devastating circumstances that they may invite or encounter. To the many supportive peers who realized that I possessed a valuable message that millions desperately need to be equipped with, and who bugged me to finish this book, thank you. Embrace this critical insight into what you or your loved ones may need to know when and if confronted with an incident that escalates and results in actually being taken to jail.

Special thanks to my wife who urged me to be shameless and to boldly empower others with my testimony. Additional thanks to all the Ministers, professors, former employers, and correctional officers, who played significant roles in helping me to go through and grow through the processes that made the first edition of this book a great tool for both consoling and curriculums.

References

Baldas, T. (2020, January 31). Detroit mom, activist forced to give birth in shackles cuts deal to go free. *Detroit Free Press*. https://www.freep.com/story/news/local/michigan/detroit/2020/01/31/siwatu-salama-ra-prison-gun/2860460001/

Berryessa, C.M. (2018). Potential impact of research on adolescent development on juvenile judge decision-making and sentencing. Juvenile and Family Court Journal 69, no. 3, 19-38.

Ciaramella, C. (2021, November 16). Cops thought sand from her stress ball was cocaine. She spent nearly 6 months in jail. https://reason.com/2021/11/16/cops-thought-sand-from-her-stress-ball-was-cocaine-she-spent-nearly-6-months-in-jail/

Clark, M. (2021, August 1). U.S. Department of Justice publishes statistics on prisoners' deaths. *Prison Legal News*. https://www.prisonlegalnews.org/news/2021/aug/1/us-department-justice-publishes-statistics-prisoners-deaths/

Cowen, A. (2017, September 5). Self-report captures 27 distinct categories of emotion bridged by continuous gradients. *Proc Natl Acad Sci USA*. 114(38): E7900-E7909. doi:10.1073/pnas.1702247114

Fleming, I., Baum, A., & Weiss, L. (1987). Social density and perceived control as mediator of crowding stress in high-density residential neighborhoods. *Journal of Personality and Social Psychology*, 52, 899–906. (p. 539)

Gerber, C. (2021, December 13). Bobby Bostic to be released from prison next year. *The Missouri Times.* https://jlc.org/news/bobby-bostic-be-released-prison-next-year

Gross, S. (2015, July 24). The staggering number of wrongful convictions in America. *The Washington Post.* https://www.washingtonpost.com/opinions/the-cost-of-convicting-the-innocent/2015/07/24/260fc3a2-1aae-11e5-93b7-5eddc056ad8a_story.html

Gutschke, L. (2021, December 15). Driver sentenced after pleading guilty in deaths of 2 girls in Interstate 20 crash. Abilene Reporter-News. https://www.reporternews.com/story/news/crime/2021/12/15/shelby-buchanan-serve-jail-time-deaths-2-girls-i-20-abilene-crash-clyde-lindley-sisters/8910051002/

Hallett, M. & Johnson, B. (2021, October 25). A church without walls, behind walls: How Evangelicals are transforming American prisons. Public Discourse Journal of the Witherspoon Institute. https://www.thepublicdiscourse.com/2021/10/78662/

Ians. (2022, January 14). Indian American man jailed for selling stolen Apple products. Telangana Today. https://telanganatoday.com/indian-american-man-jailed-for-selling-stolen-apple-products#:~:text=San%20Francisco%3A%20Indian%2DAmerican%20Saurabh,to%2066%20months%20in%20prison.

Knapp, A. (2020, September 14). Report: Dylann Roof attacker's jail cell was unlocked for 12 hours; no formal reprimands given. *The Post and Courier.*

https://www.postandcourier.com/church_shooting/report-dylann-roof-attackers-jail-cell-was-unlocked-for-12-hours-no-formal-reprimands-given/article_39d5ee4c-e709-11e6-b4ac-b32a5368e884.html

Lukitsch, B. (2021, December 1). Kansas City woman gets 5 years for passing mail to prison ordering murder of inmate. *The Kansas City Star*. https://www.kansascity.com/news/local/crime/article256264792.html#storylink=cpy

Maryland trio set free after being wrongfully jailed for 36 years. (2019, November 26). BBC News. https://www.bbc.com/news/world-us-canada-50557396

Pewter Research Center. (2012, March 22). Religion in prisons-A 50 state survey of prison chaplains. https://www.pewresearch.org/religion/2012/03/22/prison-chaplains-exec/

Rodin J. (1986). Aging and health: Effects of the sense of control. *Science (New York, N.Y.)*, *233*(4770), 1271–1276. https://doi.org/10.1126/science.3749877

Sawyer, W. & Wagner, P. (2020, March 24). Mass incarceration: The whole pie 2020. Prison Policy Initiative. https://www.prisonpolicy.org/reports/pie2020.html#

The Annie E. Casey Foundation. (2021). Youth incarceration in the United States. https://www.aecf.org/resources/youth-incarceration-in-the-united-states

Umez, C. & Pirius, R. (2018). Barriers to work: People with criminal records. National Conference of State Legislatures. https://www.ncsl.org/research/labor-and-employment/barriers-to-work-individuals-with-criminal-records.asp

U.S. Department of Justice (2018, May 15). Florida man who assaulted airline flight crew and passengers sentenced to two years in prison. https://www.justice.gov/usao-wdwa/pr/florida-man-who-assaulted-airline-flight-crew-and-passengers-sentenced-two-years-prison

U.S. Department of Justice (2022, Jan 13). Former Corrections officer sentenced to 3 years for smuggling drugs and cell phones into state prison. https://www.justice.gov/usao-sdca/pr/former-corrections-officer-sentenced-3-years-smuggling-drugs-and-cell-phones-state

eWinters, K. C., & Arria, A. (2011). Adolescent brain development and drugs. *The prevention researcher*, *18*(2), 21–24.

146

www.ingramcontent.com/pod-product-compliance
Lightning Source LLC
Chambersburg PA
CBHW032058020426
42335CB00011B/398